501
Writing Prompts

501

Writing Prompts

LearningExpress ®

NEW YORK

Library of Congress Cataloging-in-Publication Data:
501 writing prompts.— 1st ed.
        p. cm.—(LearningExpress skill builder in focus)
    ISBN 1-57685-438-8 (pbk.)
    1. English language—Rhetoric—Examinations—Study guides. 2. Report writing—
        Examinations—Study guides. I. LearningExpress (Organization) II. Series.
    PE1408 .A15 2003
    808'.042'076—dc21

                                                        2002151698

Printed in the United States of America

9 8 7 6 5 4

First Edition

ISBN 1-57685-438-8

For more information or to place an order, contact LearningExpress at:
    55 Broadway
    8th Floor
    New York, NY 10006

Or visit us at:
    www.learnatest.com

The LearningExpress Skill Builder in Focus Writing Team is comprised of experts in test preparation, as well as educators and teachers who specialize in language arts and math.

LearningExpress Skill Builder in Focus Writing Team

Lara Bohlke
Middle School Math Teacher,
  Grade 8
Dodd Middle School
Cheshire, Connecticut

Elizabeth Chesla
English Instructor
Coordinator of Technical &
  Professional Communication
  Program
Polytechnic University, Brooklyn
South Orange, New Jersey

Brigit Dermott
Freelance Writer
English Tutor, New York Cares
New York, New York

Darren Dunn
English Teacher
Riverhead School District
Riverhead, New York

Cindy Estep
Math Instructor
South Shore Christian School,
  Long Island, New York
Linganore High School,
  Frederick, Maryland
Adjunct Professor,
  Frederick Community College,
Frederick, Maryland

Barbara Fine
English Instructor
Secondary Reading Specialist
Setauket, New York

Sandy Gade
Project Editor
LearningExpress
New York, New York

Melinda Grove
Adjunct Professor, Quinnipiac
  University and Naugatuck Valley
    Community College
Middle School Math Teacher,
  Grade 8
Dodd Middle School
Cheshire, Connecticut

Noah Kravitz
Educational Technology Specialist
Brooklyn, New York

Kerry McLean
Project Editor
Math Tutor
Shirley, New York

Meg Moyer
Math Teacher, Vestal Central High
  School
Vestal Central School District
Vestal, New York

William Recco
Middle School Math Teacher,
  Grade 8
Shoreham/Wading River School
  District
Math Tutor
St. James, New York

Colleen Schultz
Middle School Math Teacher,
  Grade 8
Vestal Central School District
Math Tutor
Vestal, New York

Contents

Introduction   ix

1   Persuasive Writing Prompts   1
        Rubrics—Scoring Explanations   19
        Model Persuasive Essays   20

2   Expository Writing Prompts   51
        Rubrics—Scoring Explanations   60
        Model Expository Essays   61

3   Narrative Writing Prompts   89
        Rubrics—Scoring Explanations   102
        Model Narrative Essays   103

4   Literary Response Prompts   131
        Rubrics—Scoring Explanations   144
        Model Literary Response Essays   145

Introduction

Welcome to *501 Writing Prompts*! This book is designed to provide you with a variety of writing topics and model essays. Categories in this book cover many different types of writing: persuasive, expository, narrative, and literary response. At some point in your life, whether you are trying to pass an academic exam or standardized test, writing a college placement essay, or vying for a job promotion, you will need to practice the skills used to express yourself clearly.

How to Use This Book

First, decide on the type of essay you will need to write. There are four types of writing that are commonly used in a given situation. **Persuasive writing** argues a point and is often called argumentation. When you write persuasively, you are always expressing an opinion. In order to convince your reader, you must be able to present sound reasons and good examples. For instance, instead of explaining the causes of the Civil War, you might be asked to persuade your reader that the Civil War was more about the economics of the southern plantation system than the social issue of slavery. Persuasive writing and language is often found in editorials, letters of complaint, or proposals. **Expository writing** is explanatory. You select information from oral, written, or electronic text and organize it to show that you understand a concept. Expository writing is the type of writing you create for term papers, essays, or letters. Most standardized tests often include an expository prompt. **Narrative writing** is a type of writing that requires you to tell a story that describes an event or relates a personal experience. A good narrative should have convincing characters, a plot, and a theme. You may be asked to write a narrative of personal experience on your college placement essay. If you write a **literary response** essay, you will have to read and analyze a piece of literature and then make comments based on the literal and implied interpretations of the text. If you are taking a state assessment test, you may find yourself facing a literary response essay.

Second, learn how to score your essay. For your reference, there is a scoring guide—often called a rubric—in each chapter of this book. To determine your score, simply refer to the categories on the scoring guide to see how your writing measures up. If you have difficulty figuring out your score, ask someone knowledgeable, like a teacher, counselor, writing coach, college professor, or even your boss, to help you.

And last, check some of the model essays provided in this book. There are sample essays available for all of the bold-faced prompts throughout the book. The samples provide a look at a top essay, a middle-of-the road essay, and a low-scoring essay. You can use these as benchmarks to compare and contrast your writing.

Make a Commitment

If you are willing to practice your writing skills, you have already taken an important step toward improving your writing. As you work through some of the prompts in this book, you may feel confident in your attempts. However, if you feel that you need more instruction before you tackle some of these writing assignments, refer to some of the other LearningExpress titles: *Better Writing Right Now, Express Yourself, 501 Grammar and Writing Questions, Research & Writing Skills Success in 20 Minutes a Day*, or *Getting Down to Business*. A basic knowledge of language will also help you become a better writer. Use these books to get the extra practice you need: *501 Vocabulary Questions, 501 Synonyms and Antonyms, 501 Word Analogies, Goof-Proof Spelling*, or *Goof-Proof Grammar*.

501
Writing Prompts

Persuasive Writing Prompts

Choose one of the persuasive writing prompts from the list below and write an essay. A certain number of prompts have model essays in the answer section that you can use to compare and contrast your writing. A scoring guide, or rubric, is also included in the answer section. You can use this guide to give you an idea of the way your essay may be graded. If you have trouble interpreting the scoring guide, see a teacher or professor for help. Sample responses to the prompts in bold can be found at the end of the section.

1. Many people believe that television violence has a negative effect on society because it promotes violence. Do you agree or disagree? Use specific reasons and examples to support your response.

2. According to some people, elderly drivers should be required to reapply for their driving licenses because with age comes diminished vision, hearing, and reaction time. How do you feel about this issue? Explain what you think should be done and why.

3. Medical researchers, cosmetic companies, and others often perform experiments on animals. Many people feel that experimentation on animals is wrong and should be stopped immediately because animals do feel pain, and there are other alternatives. How do you feel? State your position and explain your reasons.

4. In order to save money, your principal is thinking about canceling all field trips for the remainder of the year. Write an essay persuading him or her to allow students to continue attending field trips. Use specific reasons and examples to support your response.

5. Some people are actively involved in promoting and supporting a cause, such as the release of international political prisoners or protecting the environment. Is there a cause you actively support? Write an essay convincing readers to support that cause.

6. Since the cloning of the sheep Dolly, there has been much debate over whether or not human beings should be cloned. Many people feel this is a violation of the natural order of things and that all research in the area of human cloning should be banned. Others feel that this is a natural progression of science and human evolution and that research in the area of human cloning should be a priority. How do you feel about this issue? Use specific reasons and examples to support your position.

7. **Many parents give children a weekly or monthly allowance regardless of their behavior because they believe an allowance teaches children to be financially responsible. Other parents only give children an allowance as a reward for completing chores or when they have behaved properly. Explain what you think parents should do and why.**

8. Many people volunteer their time to help others, either through non-profit organizations, churches, or other charitable venues. Write an essay convincing readers to find a charity and volunteer their time.

9. All-girl schools have been gaining popularity in recent years because of the belief that girls learn better when they aren't competing with or intimidated by boys, who statistically get more attention in the classroom. Do you think single-sex schools are a good idea? Why or why not? Use specific reasons and examples to support your position.

10. We all have favorite activities that we enjoy. Write an essay convincing readers to try the activity that you enjoy most.

11. Research shows that the average American watches as much as six hours of television each day. Do you think this is too much? Write an essay convincing readers to spend less time in front of the TV.

12. Many junior high and high schools around the country now require students to spend a certain number of hours each term doing volunteer work or community service. Some people believe this is an excellent idea that promotes good citizenship and cultivates compassion. Others feel that forced volunteerism is not volunteerism at all. How do you feel about this issue? Use specific reasons and examples to support your position.

13. Most states allow people to get a driver's license at the age of 16. Some people feel that 16 is much too young for the responsibility that comes with driving a car and that teenagers should not be allowed to drive until the age of 18. In your opinion, at what age should people be allowed to drive, and why?

14. As part of the "war on drugs" and in reaction to an increase in school violence, many schools across the nation now conduct targeted searches of student lockers and backpacks. Although the Supreme Court has ruled that public school officials have the right to search students' persons and property when they have reasonable cause to suspect weapons or drugs, many people feel this is a gross violation of students' right to privacy. Others feel that since school officials are responsible for the well-being of students while they are in the building, they have the right to search for drugs or weapons at any time. How do you feel about this issue? State your position and explain your reasons with specific examples.

15. Write an essay convincing readers to break a specific habit that is harmful to their physical, emotional, or financial health.

16. In many countries, citizens are required to serve in the military for a year or more. Do you believe the United States should institute a similar practice? Why or why not? Use specific reasons and examples to support your answer.

17. Have you ever traveled to a place that you found very meaningful and rewarding? Write an essay that persuades others to visit this important place.

18. Many of us spend hours in front of our computers and communicate more by e-mail or instant-messaging than in person. Some people believe that this is good because it helps shy people communicate more openly with others. Others believe that computer communication prevents us from developing interpersonal skills and limits our ability to have meaningful relationships with others. How do you feel about this issue? Use specific reasons and examples to support your position.

19. Some companies offer a paternity leave that allows fathers to stay home with their newborns for several weeks while still earning partial pay and benefits. Do you think this is a good policy? Why or why not? Explain your answer.

20. According to some health organizations, many foods on our grocery store shelves are made with genetically modified ingredients. Most of these foods, however, do not have a GMO (genetically modified organism) label. Do you think there should be a law requiring manufacturers to label foods containing GMOs? Use specific reasons and examples to support your position.

21. **More and more farmers and food manufacturers are genetically modifying their crops to reduce susceptibility to disease, improve flavor, and reduce costs. Do you think genetically modifying foods is a good idea? Why or why not? Use specific reasons and examples to support your position.**

22. A few decades ago, many families had half a dozen or more children. Nowadays, more and more families are choosing to have only one or two children. Are smaller families better than larger ones? Why or why not? State your position and support it with specific reasons and examples.

23. Representatives of credit card companies can often be found on college campuses offering special incentives to get students to fill out credit card applications. Many people feel that this takes advantage of students, who are often low on cash during their college years. Others feel that it is an excellent way to help students begin to build credit and learn financial responsibility. How do you feel about this issue? Take a position and use specific reasons and examples to support your argument.

24. Good habits improve our physical, emotional, and/or financial health. Select one of your good habits and write an essay persuading readers to make that habit a part of their lives.

25. What is your all-time favorite movie and why? Write an essay persuading readers to watch this film.

26. Today, there are more and more reality shows on television. Do these shows make good television? Why or why not? Explain your answer using specific reasons and examples.

27. Is "an eye for an eye" a good basis for determining an appropriate punishment? Why or why not? Use specific reasons and examples to explain your position.

28. Many cities suffer from serious air and noise pollution—as well as endless traffic jams—because of too many cars. Some people feel that cities with extensive public transportation systems should ban passenger cars and force people to walk, bike, or use public transportation. Do you think this is a good idea? Why or why not?

29. On today's talk shows, guests and audience members often argue heatedly with each other, and on more than one occasion, guests and audience members have been hurt. Do today's talk shows go too far? Explain your answer.

30. Have you ever made a change that improved your life or the lives of others? Write an essay that convinces readers to make a change for the better.

31. The singer and songwriter Bob Dylan once wrote, "A man is a success if he gets up in the morning and gets to bed at night and in between does what he wants to do." Do you agree with this definition of success? Why or why not? Use specific reasons and examples to support your position.

32. Carpooling, recycling, and planting trees are all activities that are good for the environment. Write an essay convincing readers to actively participate in one of these activities.

33. The Internet includes many websites with images and content that are inappropriate. Should websites like these be censored by parents? Why or why not? State your position and support it with specific reasons and examples.

34. Some people prefer to live in the quiet of the country; others prefer the hustle and bustle of the city. Which do you think is the better choice? State your position and support it with specific reasons and examples.

35. Is there a book that you feel should be required reading for everyone? Write an essay persuading your audience to read this book.

36. Some people go right on to college after high school; others take a year or more off to work or travel. Which do you think is the better choice? State your position and support it with specific reasons and examples.

37. **Some people think of the United States as a nation of "couch potatoes." Write an essay persuading readers to be more physically active.**

38. You have been asked to write a brochure to attract visitors to your hometown. Write an essay that convinces people to visit the place where you live.

39. Many states have increased the speed limit from 55 miles per hour to 65 miles per hour or more on major turnpikes and thruways. Do you think it is wise to allow motorists to drive over 65 miles per hour? Why or why not? Explain your position using specific reasons and examples.

40. **Nowadays, the private life of a politician is hardly private. In your opinion, should we be so concerned with the private affairs of a politician or political candidate? State your position and support it with specific reasons and examples.**

41. **Today's top professional athletes often have salaries and bonuses in the tens of millions of dollars. Do you think these athletes deserve such high compensation? Why or why not? Explain your position and use specific reasons and examples.**

42. Many parents do not allow their children to play with toy guns. In your opinion, is this a wise decision? Explain what you think parents should do about toy guns and why.

43. For centuries, people have wondered about the possibility of life on other planets in the universe. Do you believe extraterrestrial life exists? Write an essay persuading others to share your point of view.

44. Many science fiction stories deal with the possibility of being able to "design" our children by choosing the specific physical and personality traits we would like them to have. Do you think this is a good idea? Why or why not? Use specific reasons and examples to support your position.

45. If someone discovered a formula that would enable us to live forever, would that be a blessing or a curse? Use specific reasons and examples to support your answer.

46. Some educators argue that every child in every school should have access to computers. Others believe that the value of computers in the classroom is overrated and that computers may actually interfere with the learning process. In your opinion, how important are computers in the classroom? Use specific reasons and examples to explain your answer.

47. Should the United States invest more time, money, and effort in space exploration? Why or why not? Use specific reasons and examples to explain your position.

48. Some people believe that students aren't learning enough in high school. Should school standards be higher? Explain your answer using specific reasons and examples.

49. It has often been said, "Ignorance is bliss," and "What you don't know won't hurt you." Do you agree with these statements? Why or why not?

50. Although foreign aid spending is typically only a very small portion of our annual budget (currently about .1% of the Gross National Product), the United States still spends billions of dollars a year on foreign aid. Some people feel this is too much and that we should spend nearly all of our money addressing problems here at home. Others feel it is not nearly enough and that we should spend a great deal more helping other nations. How do you feel about this issue? Explain what you think we should do and why.

51. Some people fish to eat what they catch; others fish simply for the "sport," returning the fish to the water after they've caught it. Many animal rights activists argue that sport fishing is cruel and should be abolished. How do you feel about this issue? State your position and support it with specific reasons and examples.

52. Many schools employ security guards and have installed security equipment such as video cameras and metal detectors in the building. In your opinion, how should security in public schools be handled? Use specific reasons and examples to support your answer.

53. Across the country, public places such as libraries and museums are now smoke-free environments, and restaurants are required to have separate smoking and non-smoking sections. Some smoke-free advocates are now campaigning to ban smoking in all restaurants and bars. Do you think this is a good idea? Why or why not? Use specific reasons and examples to support your position.

54. In a small minority of schools across the nation, students do not earn grades; rather, they receive regular written and oral evaluations of their work. Some people believe that this is more effective for learning than the grading system, which they believe rewards students unevenly and encourages a competitiveness that is counterproductive to learning. How do you feel about this issue? Use specific reasons and examples to support your answer.

55. **Is reading fiction a waste of time? Why or why not? Explain your answer using specific reasons and examples to support your position.**

56. Many schools offer students who are native speakers of another language the opportunity to take classes in their native tongue so that they can more easily assimilate and better understand the material. Some educators believe that this is a disservice and that these students should be immersed in the English language. How do you feel about this issue? Use specific reasons and examples to support your position.

57. Many people immigrate to the United States because they believe that it is better than their native country. In fact, many people believe that the United States is the best country in the world. Do you agree? Why or why not?

58. Some people think that school cafeterias should be required to provide low-fat and/or vegetarian lunch options to accommodate the eating habits of all students. Do you agree or disagree? Explain your position and use specific reasons and examples as support.

59. Elementary and secondary schools around the country are beginning to actively address the problem of bullies. In your opinion, is bullying an issue that should be addressed by schools or left to parents? Use specific reasons and examples to support your position.

60. Most private schools require students to wear uniforms. Should public school students wear uniforms too? Argue for or against school uniforms for public school students. Use specific reasons and examples to support your position.

61. Do you think that the movie and/or TV ratings systems are effective or useful? Use specific reasons and examples to support your position.

62. Many people believe that honesty is the best policy. In your opinion, is it ever okay to lie? Explain your answer using specific reasons and examples.

63. In order to solve your school's recent litter problem, your principal asked students to take better care of the campus, but the litter problem continued. Your principal's reaction is to cancel all extracurricular activities until the problem is resolved. Do you agree or disagree with his reaction? Use specific reasons and examples to support your position.

64. If an alumnus donated a large sum of money to your school, how do you think that money should be spent? Write an essay convincing school officials to allocate the money in the way you think is best for the school.

65. Many people feel that American society is too competitive. Do you agree? If so, is this a good thing or a bad thing? Use specific reasons and examples to support your answer.

66. If it were up to you to choose one item from the twenty-first century to place in a time capsule for future generations, what would you choose? Use specific reasons and examples to support your choice, explaining both the item's significance and the reasons why it embodies the culture of the early twenty-first century.

67. Who makes a better leader: someone who is loved, or someone who is feared? Take a position and explain your answer.

68. Some people are concerned that many teachers are not sufficiently qualified for the classroom and argue that they should be required to pass competency tests before they are allowed to teach. Do you agree? Why or why not? Explain your answer with specific reasons and examples.

69. If it were up to you to choose one professional (a doctor, a reporter, a scientist, a politician, an actor) to travel aboard the next space station, who would you choose and why? Use specific reasons and examples to support your choice.

70. In our increasingly global society, many people feel that all students should be required to learn a foreign language before graduating from high school. Do you agree? Why or why not? Explain your position using specific reasons and examples.

71. Today, more and more colleges and universities are offering not only individual courses but entire degree programs online. Some educators worry that online programs do not provide the same quality as an on-campus education and that in an online program, students can get others to do their work. Others believe online courses offer convenience and flexibility enabling students, who might otherwise not be able, to earn a degree and complete their educations. In your opinion, should colleges and universities offer degrees entirely online? Why or why not?

72. Is a good education a right or a privilege? Why do you think so? Use specific reasons and examples to explain your answer.

73. The network that runs your favorite television show has suddenly decided to cancel it. Write a letter convincing the station to continue running the show.

74. What would improve your hometown? Write an essay convincing town officials to make a change that would improve your neighborhood.

75. Many people complain that American news shows focus too much on sensational items, such as local crimes and celebrity gossip, and spend too little time on important national and international news. In your opinion, should television news devote more time and coverage to international news and global issues? Why or why not?

76. Most students enjoy the long stretch of summer vacation, but some parents and educators feel that two and a half months is too long a break from school. Some argue that students and families would be better served if the school year were extended through July, with a three or four-week break in August, a longer winter break, and a week off each in the spring and fall. Does this sound like a good idea to you? Why or why not? Explain your answer.

77. **Many people feel that the use of surveillance cameras in public places, such as parking lots, is a good idea that can help ensure our safety. Others worry that too many cameras violate our right to privacy and give law enforcement officials too much power. In your opinion, should we install more surveillance cameras in public places? Why or why not? Support your position with specific reasons and examples.**

78. It has often been said, "a little knowledge is a dangerous thing." Do you agree? Why or why not? Use specific reasons and examples to explain your answer.

79. Recent studies have shown that students often perform better on exams if classical music is played softly in the background. However, some students may find the music distracting. Should schools play classical music during exams and/or allow students to listen to it on headphones? Take a position and explain your answer.

80. All across the country, state laws require drivers to wear seatbelts. Not everyone believes the use of seatbelts should be mandatory. What do you think? Make a case for or against mandatory seatbelt use. Use specific reasons and examples to support your position.

81. Most schools require students to read "old" texts such as ancient Greek tragedies or Shakespearian plays. Many students wonder why they should read these texts instead of more contemporary material. Make a case for or against the reading of classical literature in English classes.

82. Should a parent be a child's disciplinarian, or a child's best friend? Take a position and explain your answer using specific reasons and examples.

83. More and more Americans are deciding to eliminate meat from their diets and become vegetarians. Do you think this is a good idea? Argue for or against becoming a vegetarian. Use specific reasons and examples to support your position.

84. With the current popularity of sport utility vehicles many people believe that it's more important than ever for Congress to pass legislation requiring automobile manufacturers to use more fuel-efficient engines. Do you agree that such a law should be passed? Why or why not? Use specific reasons and examples to support your argument.

85. Every year, millions of people visit zoos around the world. But some people believe that zoos are inhumane and that animals should not be kept in captivity. Do you agree? Why or why not? Use specific reasons and examples to support your position.

86. Politicians come from all sorts of professional backgrounds, from lawyers and chief executive officers to actors and even professional wrestlers. On a few notable occasions, politicians with criminal backgrounds have even been elected. In your opinion, should candidates with a criminal record be allowed to run for office? Why or why not? Use specific reasons and examples to support your answer.

87. Students who don't want to do their homework can find dozens of sites on the Internet that offer essays for sale. Do you think this is a legitimate business, or should these enterprises be shut down? Use specific reasons and examples to support your answer.

88. Do you think the SAT or ACT exam is an accurate measure of a student's aptitude for college? Support your position with specific examples.

89. It has often been said that we can lie with silence as well as with words. Do you agree? Why or why not? Explain your answer.

90. Many students complain about having to learn history. Why do we need knowledge of the past? Write an essay convincing skeptics that learning about the past is important.

91. Woodrow Wilson once said, "Friendship is the only cement that will hold the world together." Do you agree? Use specific reasons and examples to explain your answer.

92. Charles Simmons said, "Live only for today, and you ruin tomorrow." Do you agree? Why or why not? Explain your answer.

93. Thomas Edison, the renowned inventor, is famous for having said, "Genius is one percent inspiration, ninety-nine percent perspiration." Do you agree with this definition of genius? Why or why not?

94. Many of us are fond of music that speaks to our particular generation. Write an essay that convinces others *not* in your generation that your music is worth listening to.

95. Alexander Smith said, "The great man is the man who does a thing for the first time." Do you agree with this definition of greatness? Why or why not?

96. The eighteenth century writer Samuel Johnson wrote, "Ignorance, when voluntary, is criminal." Do you agree? Use specific reasons and examples to explain your answer.

97. For decades, elementary school children across the country had been required to stand and say the Pledge of Allegiance to the American flag every school-day morning. That practice has recently been called into question, and standing and reciting the pledge is now voluntary. In your opinion, should students be required to say the pledge, should it remain voluntary, or should the practice be completely abandoned? State your position and use specific reasons and examples to support it.

98. Currently, Americans pay taxes based upon how much they earn: the higher their income, the higher the percentage of that income they must pay in taxes. Many people have been arguing that a flat tax, in which everyone pays the same rate regardless of income, would be a more equitable and desirable tax system. Which of these two tax systems do you think is best, and why? Use specific reasons and examples to support your answer.

99. The great inventor Charles F. Kettering said, "The price of progress is trouble." Do you agree with Kettering's assessment of progress? Why or why not? Use specific reasons and examples to support your answer.

100. The writer Thomas Mann said, "War is only a cowardly escape from the problems of peace." Do you agree with this claim? Why or why not? Use specific reasons and examples to support your answer.

101. Activist Jeannette Rankin once said, "You can no more win a war than you can win an earthquake." Do you agree with this statement? Why or why not? Use specific reasons and examples to support your answer.

102. Write an essay explaining why you should be admitted to a particular college.

103. The Roman leader Seneca said, "A great fortune is a great slavery." Do you agree with this claim? Why or why not? Use specific reasons and examples to support your answer.

104. If your readers were to learn a foreign language, which language do you think they should learn, and why? Write an essay convincing readers to learn that particular language.

105. Many albums and CDs now contain stickers warning parents that the lyrics of some of the songs may not be suitable for children. Some people argue that simply putting a sticker on a label is not enough. What do you think the record industry should do to warn parents about inappropriate lyrics? Explain what you think should be done and why.

106. Should we devote time and money to building a space station on the moon or Mars? Why or why not? Explain your answer.

107. **Should people lease or buy new cars? Make a case for the option that you think is best. Use specific reasons and examples to support your position.**

108. **The inventor and statesman Benjamin Franklin said, "Money never made a man happy yet, nor will it. There is nothing in its nature to produce happiness." Do you agree with this statement? Why or why not? Use specific reasons and examples to support your position.**

109. **Some states have now made it illegal to drive while talking on a hand-held cellular phone. Do you think this is a good law that should be passed in other states as well? Why or why not? Explain your answer.**

110. The poet W. H. Auden wrote, "Machines are beneficial to the degree that they eliminate the need for labor, harmful to the degree that they eliminate the need for skill." Do you agree? Why or why not? Use specific reasons and examples to explain your answer.

111. Are students learning enough science in high school? Argue for or against an expanded science requirement in secondary schools.

112. According to an old Greek proverb, "All things good to know are difficult to learn." Do you agree? Why or why not? Use specific reasons and examples to explain your answer.

113. William Hazlitt wrote, "Man is a make-believe animal—he is never so truly himself as when he is acting a part." Do you agree? Explain your answer using specific reasons and examples.

114. Imagine that you have a relative who is unfamiliar with computers and has never been on the Internet. Write an essay convincing this relative to get a computer and get online.

115. Imagine that you have found a great apartment to share, but your new roommate doesn't want any pets. Write an essay persuading your roommate to let you bring your pet with you.

116. According to a Czechoslovakian proverb, "Better a lie that soothes than a truth that hurts." Do you agree? Why or why not? Use specific reasons and examples to explain your answer.

117. Imagine that your high school (or alma mater) has decided to do away with a club to which you belong (or used to belong). Write an essay persuading school officials not to disband that organization.

118. "Original" fairy tales, like those recorded by the Brothers Grimm, often contain violence. Some literary critics and child psychologists believe these tales are good for children because they address children's real fears, feelings, and desires. Others argue that contemporary "sanitized" fairy tales still convey the main themes of the tales and are far more appropriate for children. How do you feel about this issue? Use specific reasons and examples to explain your answer.

119. Imagine that you have made it to the final round of interviews for a new job. Convince your prospective employers that you are the one who most deserves the position.

120. Most high school schedules include a study hall period several times a week. Is study hall a waste of time, or a necessary break from class? State your position and use specific reasons and examples to support your position.

121. Imagine that you have a friend who doesn't have any money in his or her savings account. Convince this friend that it's important to create and follow through with a savings plan.

122. During the Christmas holiday season, images of Santa Claus are everywhere, and young children often line up to take pictures with adults dressed as Santa. Some people feel that children should not be led to believe that Santa Claus is real. Do you agree? Why or why not? Use specific reasons and examples to support your position.

123. Is there something that you believe is truly worth fighting for? Write an essay persuading others that this cause is worth a fight.

124. Write an essay convincing your best friend to try your favorite brand of junk food.

125. Imagine that you have been asked to help raise money for a local charity. Choose a charity and write an essay convincing readers to contribute to the fundraising campaign.

RUBRIC FOR PERSUASIVE WRITING

Score	6	5	4	3	2	1
	For a grade at this level, your writing:	For a grade at this level, your writing:	For a grade at this level, your writing:	For a grade at this level, your writing:	For a grade at this level, your writing:	For a grade at this level, your writing:
Content: Your written response shows an understanding and interpretation of the writing prompt.	■ satisfies the requirements of the writing prompt in a creative and original manner. ■ uses a clear thesis statement. ■ proves the thesis with insightful examples and details.	■ provides a thoughtful analysis of the writing prompt. ■ provides a clear thesis statement. ■ offers good examples to confirm the thesis statement.	■ meets some of the requirements of the prompt. ■ includes some key elements that help explain the thesis.	■ offers a simple interpretation of the writing prompt. ■ lacks a thesis from which to base the essay.	■ meets few of the requirements of the writing prompt. ■ discusses very basic ideas. ■ makes few connections to help explain the thesis.	■ minimally addresses the writing prompt. ■ digresses, repeats, or dwells on insignificant details throughout.
Development: Your written response gives a clear and logical explanation of ideas, using supporting material.	■ builds and elaborates thoroughly. ■ uses examples precisely. ■ develops the topic in an interesting and imaginative way. ■ demonstrates coherence in the development of ideas.	■ develops the topic in an acceptable way. ■ uses relevant examples throughout the essay. ■ develops ideas clearly and consistently.	■ answers the question in an abbreviated manner. ■ gives brief examples to explain ideas. ■ develops ideas somewhat inconsistently.	■ shows weakness in the development of ideas and/or develops ideas without thorough explanation.	■ contains inaccurate, vague, or repetitive details. ■ has limited development of ideas.	■ shows a lack of development of ideas.
Organization: Your written response shows a coherent, orderly, well-reasoned approach.	■ sets up and maintains a clear focus. ■ establishes a logical, rational sequence of ideas with transitional words and sentences.	■ has an obvious plan of organization. ■ focuses on the thesis statement. ■ uses appropriate devices and transitions.	■ has a general focus. ■ obviously attempts organization. ■ exhibits a logical sequence of ideas.	■ does not show a logical sense of organization. ■ strays from the topic. ■ can be difficult to follow.	■ shows an attempt to create a focus. ■ digresses from the topic. ■ is disorganized.	■ is less organized than a 2-point response. ■ exhibits no organizational pattern or focus.
Language Use/ Conventions: Your written response shows a sense of audience by using effective vocabulary and varied sentence structure.	■ has vivid language, fluidity, and a sense of engagement and voice. ■ has sophisticated style of sentence structure, sentence variety, and vocabulary. ■ has essentially no errors.	■ has good control of mechanics. ■ contains some errors when using sophisticated language. ■ has a slightly lower quality of sentence structure and sentence variety. ■ shows errors when using sophisticated vocabulary only.	■ has a sense of audience. ■ uses simple sentences. ■ uses an appropriate level of vocabulary. ■ demonstrates partial control of mechanics. ■ exhibits some errors that do not interfere with comprehension.	■ uses vocabulary that is slightly below level. ■ has a vague sense of audience. ■ shows a beginner's control of the language. ■ has errors that begin to interfere with comprehension.	■ exhibits little control of the language. ■ has errors that make comprehension difficult.	■ shows minimal control of language skills. ■ may be illegible or unrecognizable as English.

A ZERO PAPER is:
■ totally unrelated to the topic.
■ filled with indecipherable words and is illegible.
■ incoherent with illogical or garbled syntax.
■ blank.

Scoring Explanations for Persuasive Writing Essays

A score of "**6**" indicates that your essay satisfies the requirements of the writing prompt in a creative and original manner, using an obvious theme and thesis throughout. Your essay provides a clear and logical explanation of your ideas and uses supporting material precisely. You thoroughly articulate your ideas in a coherent fashion, use precise examples, and develop the topic in an interesting manner. Your essay is orderly and well reasoned, with a clear focus, a logical sequence of ideas, and transitional words and sentences. The essay demonstrates a sense of audience by using effective vocabulary, varied sentence structure, and fluid, sophisticated language that is essentially without errors.

A score of "**4**" indicates that your essay meets some of the requirements of the writing prompt, including some key elements that help explain the thesis. Your essay may answer the question in an abbreviated manner, giving only brief examples and developing ideas somewhat inconsistently. You give the essay a general focus, make an obvious attempt at organization, and present your ideas in a logical sequence. The language of your essay indicates a general control of mechanics but has a slightly lower quality of sentence structure and variety than a sample 6 score. An essay of this type contains errors only when using sophisticated language.

A score of "**1**" indicates that your essay only minimally addresses the writing prompt, digressing, repeating, or dwelling on insignificant details throughout. An essay on this level shows a lack of development and exhibits no organizational pattern or focus. Your language skills may be illegible or unrecognizable as English.

Model Persuasive Writing Essays

7. Many parents give children a weekly or monthly allowance regardless of their behavior because they believe an allowance teaches children to be financially responsible. Other parents only give children an allowance as a reward for completing chores or when they have behaved properly. Explain what you think parents should do and why.

Sample 6 Score

Starting when I was about eight years old, my parents gave me a list of chores that had to be completed each week. If I did my chores, I got an allowance, a bit of change that I could use as I pleased. If I didn't do my chores, I didn't get my allowance. There was no other punishment, but no other punishment was necessary. That dollar or two a week was all the incentive I needed to help out around the house. Whether it was the latest Barbie or a six-pack of Hubba Bubba chewing gum, there was always something I wanted to buy. My parents could always count on me doing my chores.

I think that giving children an allowance for doing chores is a smart parenting move, for it accomplishes four important goals: It helps ensure that important work gets done around the house; it teaches children that they need to do their part to make things run smoothly for the whole family; it rewards children in a realistic, practical way for good behavior; and it helps teach children how to handle money.

I know that some people consider money for chores a form of bribery, and others feel that children should just do their chores anyway, without the incentive of an allowance. They argue that giving kids money for doing chores undermines the lesson that they need to help the family and do their part. I can understand that point of view, and when parents give their children too much money, it does undermine those lessons. But when the allowance is small, it is simply a modern version of the age-old practice of rewarding good behavior. Once children reach a certain age, money is an appropriate and effective reward that helps them learn how to be responsible and how to manage money. They get a sense of what things are worth and how much they have to save and spend to get what they want. And learning to save in order to purchase a desired item teaches them patience and helps children better understand the value of hard work.

Giving children money for doing chores is also a good introduction to the reality of the workplace. If they do the work, they get paid; if they don't do the work, they don't. Extra work can be rewarded with bonuses and extra praise; poor work may result in a pay cut or demotion.

It's important for parents to find the right amount to give. Too much money may make a child feel like hired help and will undermine the goal of teaching children to help simply because they are part of a family that must work together. On the other hand, too little money may make a child feel resentful, as if his or her work isn't worth anything to the household. What's an appropriate amount? It depends upon the amount of chores the child is expected to do and the child's age. If your nine-year-old is only expected to clean his or her room, a dollar a week is probably plenty. If your fourteen-year-old is expected to keep his room clean, take out the trash, water the plants, and vacuum the house, then ten dollars a week is more appropriate.

Being paid for my chores helped me have a good attitude about housework, taught me how to save money and spend it wisely, and enabled me to appreciate the hard work my parents did around the house. I'm really grateful that this was the way my parents chose to handle chores in our household.

Sample 4 Score

Should parents pay children for doing chores is a good question. My parents paid me, and my brothers and sister. I never liked doing chores, but getting an allowance each week (if I did my chores) made it not so bad. In fact, sometimes I did extra (like reorganizing the pantry) to get some extra money for something I really wanted.

I think having my allowance depend on my doing chores made me understand what it's like to work. In the "Real World," you don't get paid if you don't do your work. That's how it was in our house.

I also learned that it's hard work to keep a house going, I learned to appreciate all the hard work my mom and dad use to do. In addition, I learned how to save money. I would set aside my allowance to save up for something I wanted, like a new CD player or outfit.

In my opinion, parents should give an allowance for doing chores, but it shouldn't be too much. Children should know that they need to help no matter what. Too much money I think would make him or her feel like their hired help or something. Contrarily, too little money can make him or her feel like their help isn't worth anything to his or her parents. So finding the right amount is important.

In conclusion, giving children an allowance for doing household chores is a good idea. Children learn to work for their money and save what they earn.

Sample 1 Score

Many children they do not behave in properly, they should be punish, no getting reward. They should no be allowance anything. Chores is hard, on the contrary, there to learn for helping that's important. For the family. All to do the parts.

For me, it was vacuuming and the dusting. Every week, for Saturday or else. Forgetting the allowance, there wasn't. Only to be punish for what not to do.

Children should listen, to their parents. Its very important.

21. More and more farmers and food manufacturers are genetically modifying their crops to reduce susceptibility to disease, improve flavor, and reduce costs. Do you think genetically modifying foods is a good idea? Why or why not? Use specific reasons and examples to support your position.

Sample 6 Score

A few decades ago, manipulating genes in people, plants, and animals was just science fiction. Today, it's a reality, and genetic modification may have many positive applications in the future, including the eradication of many hereditary diseases. But like most scientific and technological advances, the genetic modification of organisms for our food supply can be as dangerous as it is beneficial. Because of the potential dangers of this technology, I think genetically altering plants and animals in the food supply is a practice that should be very tightly controlled and carefully studied before it is an accepted and common practice. Unfortunately, it may already be too late for that.

Many people don't even realize that many of their foods are genetically modified organisms (GMOs). GMOs are already prevalent in supermarkets and grocery stores across the country, but manufacturers are not required to label foods as having been made from GMOs. As a result, millions of Americans purchase and eat GMOs every day without even knowing it. Yet we don't even know if GMOs are harmful to our health. We don't really know how GMOs may affect our bodies or our ecosystem. When we mess with DNA, we may be making changes that have all sorts of dangerous repercussions, including some that we may not even realize for several generations.

One of the main concerns about GMOs is the unpredictability of the behavior of altered genes and of the bacteria, plants, and animals that interact with the altered organism. For example, a crop of corn genetically modified to be less susceptible to a particular insect may take on other unwanted characteristics due to the change. It may, for example, become *more* susceptible to another disease, or it could develop a tougher skin on its kernels, or it could decrease the crop's ability to produce vitamin E.

More frightening is the domino effect of genetically modifying foods. Any change in an organism's DNA has the potential to affect not only the organism but also anything that feeds off of it, *including us*. How do we know how GMOs might affect us on a microscopic, genetic level? We don't know, and can't know, without years of studies that track all sorts of potential outcomes over several generations.

Another fear is that transferred genes may escape from one organism into another. For example, imagine that Strain A of sweet peas was altered by adding a gene that would increase its sugar production. Through cross-pollination, this altered genetic code could enter other strains and slowly (or quickly) infect the entire sub-species. If the alteration was beneficial, this could be a good thing. But the altered gene might not act the same way in all varieties, and the change may not be a good thing in the first place, and/or it may have unintended consequences.

Genetically modifying foods is a practice that has been driven by the desire to make more food available more quickly and more cheaply than ever before. This attitude puts profit first and consumers and the environment last, and that is simply dangerous. The agribusiness needs to slow down and stop selling us GMOs until their safety is certain.

Sample 4 Score

In my opinion GMOs (genetically modified organisms) are a bad thing. Because we don't know enough about them, and they could be dangerous, we don't even know it. There needs to be more studies done before we know for sure its safe.

For example, modified genes could jump from one GMO to another GMO. Another problem is we don't know what other effects a genetic modification might have. If you change a plant to produce more sugar or something that might make its fruit sweeter it might ruin something else in the plant.

We eat GMOs even though it may not say so on the label. I'm worried because we don't know how those GMOs might affect our bodies. Who knows? Technically these are new foods that no human being has ever eaten before. It may be a small change but it's a change and it could be dangerous.

I think there should be a lot of studies to determine the safety of GMOs and I think any food that has GMO in it should have a big "GMO" label on it. We should know what we're eating and how it might affect us.

Sample 1 Score

Do I think genetically modifying foods is a good idea? No. My idea, its bad. Could be very dangerous. We don't no, its genes an noone ever did this kind of thing before. What could be the affects? You changing the plant from its foundation. What are the other changes it could be? This is scaring for me.

I like eating healthy food like soy. These make me feel like I'm putting good in my body. GMOS these make me feel like I'm putting bad in my body. I worry who is the mad scientist.

22. A few decades ago, many families had half a dozen or more children. Nowadays, more and more families are choosing to have only one or two children. Are smaller families better than larger ones? Why or why not? State your position and support it with specific reasons and examples.

Sample 6 Score

I grew up in a large family—I am the oldest of six—and I have many wonderful memories from my childhood. I am very close to most of my siblings and I treasure my relationships with them. But when I have my own family someday, it won't be as big as the one I grew up in. As much as my large family was full of love, and as much as I learned about sharing, giving, and patience, I think having too many kids puts too much pressure on the parents and the oldest children.

When I think back on my childhood, I remember playing with my siblings or grandparents. I don't remember spending a whole lot of time with my mother and father. They were always around, but they were always busy. Although they did their best to spend some quality time with each of us, there was just too much to do to keep our large family going. My mother was always cooking, cleaning, nursing, changing a diaper, shopping, or taking someone to baseball practice or a playdate. She was always tired.

My father, on the other hand, was always working. He needed overtime whenever he could get it, and weekends were always full of projects around the house. He had lots of helpers, of course, but there are only so many things kids can do. Even when we were able to get away for vacation, Mom and Dad couldn't really relax, because there were so many kids to look after.

Money was also a constant worry for my family. With so many children, our budget was always tight. Back-to-school shopping was always a stressful time; we all wanted the latest fashions, but we could only get a few things. My younger siblings lived on hand-me-downs as much as they could. We shopped at bargain stores and often got clothes that we didn't really like because they were on sale. Our house always needed repairs, and there was never enough money to keep up.

Another problem with large families is that the older siblings always end up being babysitters. Like it or not (and most of the time I didn't like it), I had to watch my younger brothers and sisters. At age six, I could change a diaper like a pro. I was getting my brothers and sisters dressed, giving them breakfast, helping them get ready for bed. I learned a lot about sharing, self-sacrifice, and responsibility at an early age, and these are important character traits that I value highly and want to instill in my children. But I also want to give them a chance to *be* children. I don't want them to have so much responsibility at such an early age.

I don't want to give the impression that I didn't have a happy childhood. I most definitely did; I was loved as much as my parents could love me, and I had wonderful fun with my brothers and sisters. But I always wanted a little more time with Mom and Dad, and I often resented having so much responsibility. I wished my mom wasn't always so tired and my dad didn't have to work so much. Because I want to be there more for my kids, because I want them to *be* kids throughout their childhood, I plan to have a much smaller family.

Sample 4

These days, more and more families have only a couple of kids, whereas, a few decades ago, families were much bigger, with sometimes as many as ten kids in the family. I grew up in one of those big families (we have six kids, and I am the oldest). I had a great childhood, but based on my experience and my family's, I would say that it's better to have a smaller family.

One reason I say this is because I was the oldest, and I sure did a lot of babysitting. My mom was always asking me to watch the kids while she went to the store or took one of the other kids somewhere. I don't blame her, if I had that many kids I sure would need a helper, too. But lots of times I felt like it wasn't fair and I didn't get to do things with my friends because I had to watch my brothers and sisters. I also had to change a lot of diapers, too—and I mean a lot!

I also think smaller families are better for another reason: because my mom and dad were always working and tired. I guess if you have a whole lot of money, then it isn't such a problem. However, we didn't, and my dad was always working, while my mom was always working around the house or running us around somewhere. I wished I could have spent more time with them, too.

I really love my family and especially both of my parents. I did have a great childhood, but I think a smaller family is easier and better, especially for the oldest child.

Sample 1 Score

Are smaller families better than larger ones? This is a big question. I have a large family. There are six kids. I am the oldest children. I have three brothers and two sisters. My youngest brother is ten years younger than me.

My mom, she has eleven brothers and sisters. My dad, he has ten brothers and sisters. They live far away from us. My parents, they had good childhood but for them all it was a lot of work.

24. Good habits improve our physical, emotional, and/or financial health. Select one of your good habits and write an essay persuading readers to make that habit a part of their lives.

Sample 6 Score

When I was fifteen, I wanted to get a job so I could buy a car when I turned sixteen. My father sat me down at the kitchen table and said, "Excellent. But only on one condition: 10% of every paycheck must go into a savings account. And you cannot touch that money except in an emergency."

"But Dad," I argued, "If I have to put 10% away, how will I ever save enough money to buy a car?"

"You'll have enough," he replied. "And you'll soon see how important it is to set money aside for savings."

I didn't believe him at the time, and in fact I often resented having to put that 10% in a separate account. But two years later when the transmission on my car blew, I didn't have to fret about coming up with the money for repairs. I was able to cover the cost easily and was back on the road in no time. It was then that I began to see the wisdom of my father's rule, which I adopted as my own. This habit has helped to give me a secure financial life, and I urge you to make this practice part of your life.

Ten percent of each paycheck may sound like a lot, and if you're on a tight budget to begin with, you might be thinking, "I just can't afford to do it." In truth, you can't afford *not* to do it. You never know when you are going to need an extra $100 or $1,000; life is full of surprises, and lots of them are expensive. You can afford to do this. In fact, you can't afford *not* to do this.

As tight as your budget may be, it's important to get started right away. If you are absolutely scraping by with every last penny going to bills, then start with just 5%, but move up to 10% as soon as you can. If you earn $500 a week, for example, put $25–$50 in your savings account each week. At first, this may mean clipping coupons, renting a movie instead of going to the theater, or pressing your own shirts instead of taking them to the cleaner. Think carefully about ways you can save just a few dollars—because just a few dollars from each paycheck is all it takes to build up a solid savings account.

The money you save will add up quickly. For example, if your annual salary is $40,000, each year, you would put $4,000 into your savings account. That still leaves you with $36,000 to cover all of your expenses. After ten years, you will have saved $40,000, plus interest. And the more money in your account, the more interest you earn, the larger your emergency fund, the more you can afford to relax later in your life.

Once you get in the habit of putting 10% of your money into savings, it won't feel like a sacrifice. The 90% that's left will be your working budget, and you won't even miss that 10% because you won't be used to spending it. Yet you will know that it is there, ready for an emergency, helping to keep you financially secure. So take my father's advice, and mine: Put a piece of each paycheck into your savings. It's a habit that's worth every penny.

Sample 4 Score

When I was 15, my dad helped me start a good habit that I still keep to this day, that is saving 10% of every paycheck. Whenever I get paid, I put 10% of that check into a savings account. I don't touch that money except for an emergency or special purchase.

I'm really grateful to my dad for helping me start this habit, though I wasn't at the time, because I wanted to buy a car and I didn't know how I could save up enough money if I didn't put it all towards the car, but he was right, I did save enough, and then I had money for repairs because I'd saved carefully.

The great thing about this habit is, once you're in it, you don't feel like there's any money missing. You use the 90% to figure out your budget, not the 100%. In just one year you can save a whole lot of money.

You're probably thinking, like I did, "I can't afford to put some of my money away, I need it all." However, you're wrong. You can afford it, and you'll be glad because you'll always have money for an emergency. So get started today!

Sample 1 Score

Good habits improve our physical, emotional, and/or financial health. I have many good habit. One, is, I saving money every month. Another, is, I excersize everyday. Also, I am eating healthy. I also do not never use the bad language.

I am pride of my good habits. What habits do you do that are good for you? Save money like me, also excersize all the time, and eat healthy. It will be wise to do.

35. Is there a book that you feel should be required reading for everyone? Write an essay persuading your audience to read this book.

Sample 6 Score

Most people know who Frankenstein is—or at least they think they do. Because of the way Mary Shelley's brilliant 1818 novel has been adapted to film, most Americans think that Frankenstein is a towering, scar-faced monster who brings terror wherever he goes. In Shelley's novel, however, the real monster is Victor Frankenstein, the scientist who is the monster's creator. In her story of how Victor Frankenstein creates the monster and what he does after the monster comes to life, Shelley conveys several timeless messages about the dangers of science, the dangers of isolation, and the importance of being a good parent. It is a novel that everyone should read.

In the story, Frankenstein, eager for glory, wants to discover the "elixir of life" so that he can have the power to bring the dead back to life. He wants to create a new race of superhuman beings and wants them to worship him like a god. He wants to unlock the secrets of nature and use that power for his own selfish goals. Shelley's novel warns us that we must be careful what we do with science—how we apply the knowledge we discover. For when Frankenstein does discover the "elixir of life," and when he does create a superhuman being, he creates a creature that is beyond his control. The creature is more powerful and more intelligent than Victor Frankenstein, and the creature engineers Frankenstein's demise.

Shelley's novel also warns us about the dangers of isolation. Frankenstein's creation is so revolting and dangerous in part because Frankenstein works completely alone. He becomes so absorbed with his project that he completely blocks out family and friends. He stops communicating with others and works secretly; he does not consult others about his project, partly because he knows that what he is doing is wrong, partly because he wants all the glory. But because he does not work with others, because he loses touch with his community of family and friends, he also loses touch with his responsibility to other human beings. When the creature comes to life, Frankenstein runs away, abandoning his creation even though he knows the creature might harm others.

This abandonment brings us to the novel's third timeless message: the importance of being a good parent. Frankenstein creates a living being and then abandons him because he is an "ugly wretch." He totally ignores his responsibility to the creature, who is born as innocent as a child, even though he is the size of a giant. The creature is abhorred by everyone he meets, and because no one has ever shown him love, he learns to hate. And the person he comes to hate most is the father who abandoned him. Shelley's message is clear: you are responsible for what you create, and if you are a parent, you must love your child, whatever his or her appearance.

In our age of cloning and genetic engineering, of scattered communities and neighbors who don't know each other's names, of abandoned children and abusive parents, Shelley's book may have more importance than ever. It is also a powerful and suspense-filled tale. Will Frankenstein capture the creature? Will he create a "bride" for the monster? Will Walton, the ship captain who records Frankenstein's story, learn from Frankenstein's tale? Find out for yourself. Grab a copy of this amazing novel and enjoy.

Sample 4 Score

Frankenstein isn't who most people think he is, which is the monster. The *real* Frankenstein is the scientist who brings the monster to life. You'd know this if you read one of the greatest novels ever written, Mary Shelley's *Frankenstein*, a book that I think everyone should read. This book is great because its suspensefull and teaches some important lessons, these lessons are maybe even more important to day than they were in Shelly's time. (Which was the 1800s.)

One lesson is about how to use science. Dr. Frankenstein in the story discovers how to bring a dead person back to life. But everything goes wrong after the creature wakes up. What was supposed to be a great thing that would bring Frankenstein all kinds of glory and make him like a master creator instead brought him and lots of other people all kinds of terrible horror. I think Mary is telling us to be very careful how we use science.

She also is telling us in this story to stay close to others. Frankenstein makes the creature all by himself. While he's working on the monster; he doesn't talk to anyone, no one in the university knows what on earth he's up to, he's got a big secret. He's so obsessed and he forgets to think about what will happen once this giant creature comes to life. He doesn't think about being responsible to and for the creature. Because he worked alone he forgot about that.

The third lesson is that we need to be good parents. Frankenstein is like the creature's father and mother. He created him, and he needs to take care of him. But he doesn't, he just runs away. That's when his horror begins, and the creature's, too. The poor creature is hated by everyone and his life is really sad.

Read this excellent book!

Sample 1 Score

Every school has required reading that all the kids are required to read for school. There are lots of different books on this list, I read some of them, some of them are good but I dont like them all.

One book that hard to read but I liked it, was, Frankenstien. The story of the monster. Frankenstin makes this monster out of dead body parts. Then he makes the monster come to life, through some secret way he doesn't tell anybody about. Then he runs away and gets attacked and becomes a killer because everyone hates him. Frankenstine, is a really good story.

37. Some people think of the United States as a nation of "couch potatoes." Write an essay persuading readers to be more physically active.

Sample 6 Score

Is your favorite place in the home sitting on the couch in front of the television? Do you spend hours and hours there each day, surrounded by bags of chips and cans of soda? Do you panic when you can't find the remote control and think that you might actually have to get up off of the sofa to change the channel?

If you answered "yes" to any of these questions, you are not alone. In fact, you are one of the millions of Americans who are "couch potatoes": people who spend their days and nights "vegging out" in front of the "tube."

Well, spud, it's time to get up out of that armchair and get some exercise! I know how seductive television can be. I know how easy it is to plop onto the sofa and lose yourself in the world of sports, reality shows, and good-old make-believe. I know how mesmerizing MTV and other channels can be and how hard it can be to pull yourself away. But all that television spells disaster for your body because it needs to be active to be healthy. And it's no good for your mental health or social life, either.

Think about what all that time in front of the television is doing to your body. Think about what all that sagging muscle and growing belly is doing to your life. Think about how your lack of energy affects you at work.

Now think about how different things would be if you spent some of that

TV time getting exercise instead: You would feel better during the day. You would sleep better at night. You would have more energy. You would look better. You would have more confidence. You would be more creative. You would be healthier and happier. And you would not even miss the television.

What sort of exercise can you do? *Anything!* Go for a walk. Ride a bike. Jog. Lift weights. Take an aerobics class. Do yoga. Join a basketball or hockey league. Swim. Roller blade. Grab a friend, a fellow couch potato, and exercise together.

You can start with just fifteen minutes a day, two or three days a week, and build up slowly. Before you know it, your couch potato days will be over, and you will wonder how on earth you ever spent so much time in front of the TV.

Sample 4 Score

Americans everywhere are "couch potatoes." These are people who just sit in front of the TV all day and night. They spend so much time on the couch they're almost becoming part of the couch. They don't ever want to get up to change the channel, so the remote control is like a part of their hand. Is that what you're like? Do you spend too much time in front of the TV? Well, it's time to stop being a couch potato. You need to take care of your body. It's time for you to get up and get some excercise.

If you lay around all day, think of how that's just not good for you. It's not healthy. You need to get excercise to be healthy. Physical activity at least three times a week will get you back in shape. It will help you have a healthy heart, better sleep, and less likely to get sick and diseases because your immune system will be stronger. Furthermore, you'll have more energy and just feel better. This is especially good for you at work. In addition, you'll be more confident because you will look better and fit into nicer clothes. When you feel better about yourself, you're happier.

Its easy to get excercise. You can do some jumping jacks or jog or play tennis. Even just walking to the store instead of driving can help. Maybe you could join a gym or a sports team, like a basketball team in your neighborhood. Or ask a friend whose also a couch potato to excercise with you. Its easier when you have someone to excercise with.

So do yourself a favor, stop spending so much time in front of the TV! You'll be proud when your days as a couch potato are over.

Sample 1 Score

For some people's thinking, there are to many "couch potatos", all across the American country. There are lying on there couchs all the time, doing nothing. Except watching the TV all the time. Whereas they not getting any excersizing, not anything at all. Theres so much to do, like jogging or walking or tennis instead.

The couch potatos, they should not be just on the couch, but also excersizing. Think about being this like a potato. Is not a good thing! Instead, to be like a lion or strong like a bull.

40. Nowadays, the private life of a politician is hardly private. In your opinion, should we be so concerned with the private affairs of a politician or political candidate? State your position and support it with specific reasons and examples.

Sample 6 Score

When you think of former president Bill Clinton, what's the first thing that comes to mind? Unfortunately, for many people, the first thing they think of is Monica Lewinsky. Like millions of people around the globe, I was horrified by how much the investigation delved into Mr. Clinton's private affairs. No one needed to know the sort of details that were revealed by Ken Starr's investigation. But while I don't want to know the details, I do believe we have a right to know what sort of lives our politicians are living. I believe their behavior in private is a reflection of their true values and how they will behave in office.

For example, if a politician lies to his or her spouse (I'm talking about big lies, like infidelity, not little white lies), that tells us something about his or her character. In my opinion, this person is not to be trusted. I wouldn't have faith that this politician would keep his or her word. True, the relationship between a husband and wife is very different from that between a politician and his or her constituents. But the politician's respect for that relationship and how he or she deals with any problems in that relationship reflects his or her level of integrity.

Similarly, if a politician (or political candidate) behaves in an illegal manner, that shows a disrespect for the law. A government official who employs an illegal resident as a nanny or housekeeper, for example, or pays a nanny or housekeeper under the table to avoid taxes is acting as if he or she is above the law—or demonstrating that he or she simply doesn't care about the law. This is not the kind of person I want in a public office.

On the other hand, if a politician leads a respectable, law-abiding life at home, we can expect a respectable, law-abiding performance in office. A politician who deals honestly with family, friends, and business associates is likely to deal honestly with his or her constituents as well. A politician who respects the law in all aspects of his or her private life is likely to respect the law while in office, too. A candidate who behaves in a cautious, reserved manner regarding his or her personal affairs is likely to bring a similar approach to the office.

I know that nobody is perfect and that every politician may have skeletons in the closet. I'm not talking about transgressions from the distant past. But I am concerned with a politician's recent past and current behavior. Is he or she honest or does he or she break promises? Does he or she behave recklessly or in a thoughtful and controlled manner? We cannot separate who we are personally from who we are professionally. That is why I believe the public has a right to know.

Sample 4 Score

Politicians live very public lives. If their big politicians (like the president, for example), they don't really have any privacy. Everybody knows everything they do. This probably bothers some people, however, I actually think that is a very good thing. I think we need to know what politicians are really like. How they are at home (in private) tells us about how they will be in the office.

It's true that we are different at home and in the office. However, we're still the same person. In other words, we will pretty much act the same, on the same values and principals, whether we're at home or in the office. If we would steal or lie at home, we would probably steal or lie in the office. So, if a politician lies to his wife, for example, or to her business partners, then we can probably expect them to lie to the people who elected them.

On the contrary, if a politician lives an honest life and always obeys the law. We can probably expect them to behave honestly and lawfully when they are in office. Because like I started to say before, you can't separate home and work. We're the same person in both places.

So, in conclusion, it's a good idea to have knowledge about politician's private affairs. They probably don't like it and want things to be private. However, since they are our elected officials, they have to be public, unfortunately for them about almost everything.

Sample 1 Score

The politicians, they have privacy in there homes. For them too much is knowed about everything what they is doing. This is bad; for them. Whereas, knowing the public are a very good thing for us. If lying and stealing there, also here. Don't you agree? It is clear. If they are a liar at home, we will be lying to also. So therefore, in my opinion, "we should be so concerned with the private affairs of a politician or political candidate."

41. Today's top professional athletes often have salaries and bonuses in the tens of millions of dollars. Do you think these athletes deserve such high compensation? Why or why not? Explain your position and use specific reasons and examples.

Sample 6 Score

When he was at the height of his basketball career, Michael Jordan was making approximately $300,000 *per game.* That's more than most people make in a year; indeed, it's more than some people earn in a lifetime. Yes, Michael Jordan was a phenomenal basketball player. Yes, he was also a fantastic role model. But no, he did not deserve to earn such a ridiculously high salary. Jordan, like many other top professional athletes, was grossly overpaid.

Why do top athletes earn such inflated salaries? Because they bring big bucks into their cities and franchises. But what sort of service do they provide to society? Do they save lives? No. Do they improve the standard of living or promote positive social change? No. Do they help keep our streets safe or educate our kids? No. True, many of the top athletes are good role models for our children. But seven-figure salaries don't always mean model behavior. Take N.B.A. star Latrell Spreewell, for example, who choked and threatened to kill his coach.

It is true that professional athletes work hard, and many have spent their lives pursuing their goals. It is also true that most professional athletes have a relatively short career span—a decade perhaps at the top of their game. Limited as their professional sporting career may be, they don't deserve such high salaries. After their professional sports careers are over, they can certainly pursue other careers and work "regular" jobs like the rest of us. Ending their stint as professional athletes doesn't mean they have to stop earning incomes. They just have to earn incomes in a different way. Why should they be any different from the rest of us who may need to switch careers?

It is also true that professional athletes may be injured while on the job; their work is indeed physical, and especially in contact sports like football, injuries are bound to happen. But, like the rest of us, they have insurance, and in nearly all cases, their exorbitant salaries more than cover their medical costs. And theirs is not the only high-risk job. What about miners, construction workers, or firefighters? They are at risk for physical injury every day, too—injuries that could likewise end their careers. But they sure aren't earning millions of dollars a year.

It is also true that professional athletes may spend years and years practicing with farm teams for a fraction of the salary they receive once they make it to the top. But in every career path, we start off with lower wages and must pay our dues and work our way up. Besides, farm team salaries are not always so low.

We're a sports-crazy country, a nation of fanatic sports fans and celebrity worshippers. We're awed and entertained by the best of them—the Michael Jordans, the Alex Rodriguezes, the Emmitt Smiths. But as much as they may inspire and amuse us, professional athletes do not deserve such high salaries. Those millions could be much more wisely spent.

Sample 4 Score

Do athletes get paid too much? You bet. That's my opinion.

Professional athletes, what do they do with all that money? Imagine Michael Jordan earning $300,000 per game! Plus all his money from Nike and other advertising. I think that money can be put to much better use in this country.

Professional athletes should get good salaries, but not the millions like they get now. It's just too much. Their job isn't dangerous, except maybe for football or ice hockey where it's easy to get a bad injury. It's easy to get a bad injury in lots of other jobs, too, like construction, but they don't get millions of dollars. I guess, the difference is that nobody likes to watch construction workers. There's fun in the game and people like the competition, sports teams bring lots of money into a city's economy.

If professional athletes could guarantee they'd also be a good role model for kids, then maybe they could have such high salaries. Because they'd be doing something good for society since so many kids are watching. For now though, it's too much.

Sample 1 Score

Today the athleets so much money. Millions an millions of the dollars. They playing baseball, basketball; football, even for golf. This is the not of the dangerous sport, even less than many of the others.

The money, it's too much, giving mine opinon. For the teems and the citys its so much there's else to pay for with the money, like homelessness. This is the need to be changed.

55. Is reading fiction a waste of time? Why or why not? Explain your answer using specific reasons and examples to support your position.

Sample 6 Score

Remember the last book that captured your imagination, that transported you to another place and time? Remember a book that made you fall in love with its characters, made you feel their pain and joy? Remember a story that taught you an important lesson, that helped you better understand others, make sense of the human condition? If so, then you can understand why the question, "Is reading fiction a waste of time?" is such a silly question.

Fiction, unlike a user manual, a magazine article, or newspaper editorial, probably won't offer you any practical knowledge that you can put to immediate use. It won't inform you of current events or give you advice on how to cultivate a better garden. It probably won't help you decide which candidate to vote for or which product to buy. But that certainly doesn't mean it's useless or impractical. Indeed, fiction serves three important functions for human beings: It helps us be more compassionate to others, it helps us better understand ourselves, and it cultivates our imaginations. It can also teach us about history, psychology, even biology and other sciences.

Compassion for others is rooted in understanding and acceptance, and a good story brings us into the inner world of its characters so that we can understand them. In Toni Morrison's novel *The Bluest Eye*, for example, Morrison peels away the layers of her characters' histories piece by piece like an onion until we see into their core and understand what drives them. They may still do awful things to each other, but she shows us *why* they do the things that they do, and we learn that we shouldn't judge others until we understand their pasts. Their stories are sad and painful, and we learn to love even the outcast Pecola. In fact, we learn that those outcasts are the ones who need our love the most.

Many stories and novels also help us better understand ourselves. Joseph Conrad's dark and powerful novel *Heart of Darkness* helps us see that all of us have a dark side, and that we need to acknowledge this dark side in order to control it. It makes us question just how civilized we are and indeed what it means to be civilized in the first place.

Good fiction also cultivates our imagination, which is more important to us than some might think. Without imagination, we live a sad, empty life. Imagination is central to our emotional health and is a key factor in our level of intelligence. Facts are one thing; but facts can be of no real use unless coupled with imagination. Fiction can help us by keeping our imagination fresh and active. In a story like Franz Kafka's "Metamorphosis," for example, we are asked to imagine that Gregor, the main character, wakes up one morning and has turned into a giant bug. Crazy? Perhaps. But once we accept this premise and imagine Gregor as a five-foot long cockroach, we can feel his family's horror and imagine his agony as he finds himself trapped in his room and abandoned by those he loves.

Is reading fiction a waste of time? That's like asking if laughing is a waste of time. We don't need fiction to survive, but we do need it to be kinder, more understanding, and more creative human beings.

Sample 4 Score

Is reading fiction a waste of time? I am surprised by this question. I never thought of it as a waste of time. I understand that it is not practical like reading a "how-to" article or something like that. However, on the other hand, it is good for you. I think it helps you have a good imagination and be a better person.

I think fiction helps you be a better person because it helps you understand people. Lots of stories help you understand why people do what they do. For example, in *The Bluest Eye*, at the end of the story we understand why the people do the things that they do. We judge the characters right away but then we learn about them and maybe change our judgment. The book was written by Toni Morrison.

Second, I think fiction also helps you understand yourself. Some stories help us see that we all have a good side and a dark side within. Fiction can also help us have a good imagination, and this is important in helping us be creative. Being creative can help you better solve problems and think of original things.

I love reading fiction, and I never think it is a waste of time. It may not be practical, like reading the newspaper, however it is a lot more fun and helps me be a better person.

Sample 1 Score

Is reading fiction a waste of time? is a question. How is the answer? Like you and me, wondering, is fun things a waste of time too, or only do the practical what you should? These be important questions. What the answer?

In my opinion, no way, Jose! It fun to read fiction stories. Its like imagenation, cool things.

So don't beleive it. Say who! Reading fiction ain't wasting time. In my opinion.

58. Some people think that school cafeterias should be required to provide low-fat and/or vegetarian lunch options to accommodate the eating habits of all students. Do you agree or disagree? Explain your position and use specific reasons and examples as support.

Sample 6 Score

It's a fact: There are students across the United States who are vegetarian and/or health conscious, and school cafeterias should be required to provide low-fat and/or vegetarian lunch options for them. Even more importantly, many teenagers' dietary decisions are not only based on health concerns but also religious and/or moral issues. In this day and age, an individual's eating habits often reflect his or her identity. For these reasons, it's imperative that each school's cafeteria menu be as diverse as its student body.

Just by reading headlines in any of the major news magazines, it becomes clear that the United States is a nation that needs to slim down. In every town and city, there are an abundance of fast food restaurants that lure teenage customers with fast, inexpensive, and tasty food, but these foods are typically unhealthy. Unfortunately, school cafeterias, in an effort to provide food that is appetizing to young people, mimic fast food menus, often serving items such as burgers and fries, pizza, hot dogs, and fried chicken. While these foods do provide some nutritional value, they are relatively high in fat, and many of them, namely burgers, hot dogs, and fried chicken, are clearly not designed for vegetarians.

Many of the lunch selections currently offered by most school cafeterias could be made vegetarian and/or more healthy with a few simple and inexpensive substitutions. Veggie burgers, for example, offered alongside beef burgers, would give both vegetarians and the health conscious more options. A salad bar woud also serve the dual purpose of providing both vegetarians and low-fat food eaters the opportunity for a satisfying meal. This is not to say that accommodating every desire or food preference is plausible, but students should have the right to be served foods that coincide with their life choices.

Sample 4 Score

In the United States there are many people who are vegetarian. In addition, there are people who choose to eat low-fat foods, either to lose weight or to stay healthy. Many of these people are students who eat lunch at their school cafeterias on a daily basis. Surprisingly though, school cafeterias are not required to provide low-fat nor vegetarian options for students.

Unfortunately, vegetarian options may be limited to the french fries (served with burgers) or pizza. While these are vegetarian (non-meat) options, they do not necesarily serve as low-fat foods. I think schools should have a wider variety of low-fat and/or vegetarian options such as a salad bar, or perhaps even something with tofu.

While cafeterias can't meet all the demands of students, it is important to offer those commited to a healthy or vegetarian lifestyle the choice. Schools should create a menu that offers these options for all students.

Sample 1 Score

Lot's of people are overwait and even fat, and the other people are vege-taran who dont eat meat. The food at schools are bad enouf and then why should they hafe to have stuff that those people like. School's shoudl have good food and meat, but not fat food for everyone.

77. Many people feel that the use of surveillance cameras in public places such as parking lots is a good idea that can help ensure our safety. Others worry that too many cameras violate our right to privacy and give law enforcement officials too much power. In your opinion, should we install more surveillance cameras in public places? Why or why not? Support your position with specific reasons and examples.

Sample 6 Score

Not long ago, the nation was gripped by the horrifying news that a baby had been stolen from a car in a parking lot while her mother, who was return-ing a shopping cart, was just a few feet away. Thanks to the description of the kidnapper captured by surveillance cameras in the parking lot and broadcast over radios, television, and highway overpass signs, the kidnap-per was quickly caught and the baby returned, unharmed, to her mother. Had it not been for those surveillance cameras, that mother would proba-bly never have seen her baby girl again.

I can't think of a much better argument for the use of surveillance cam-eras in public places. That baby's life was saved by those parking lot cameras.

Many people worry about the use of surveillance cameras in public places such as parking lots, stores, parks, and roadways. They don't like the idea that they are being watched. They worry that the information captured on the surveillance tapes can somehow be used against them. But how? It seems to me that the only reason we should worry about being caught on surveillance cameras is if we are doing something wrong. If we are behaving lawfully in a public place, then why worry if it is captured on film?

Surveillance cameras can provide two immensely important services. One, they can help us find those who commit crimes, including thieves, kidnappers, vandalizers, and even murderers. Two, they can serve as a powerful deterrent to crime. A thief who plans to steal a car may think twice if he knows he will be caught on video. A woman who hopes to kidnap a child may abandon her plans if she knows she will be captured on film.

Surveillance cameras can also help us in less critical but nonetheless practical ways. In some towns in England, for example, radio deejays use information from surveillance cameras to announce the availability of parking spaces in crowded public parking lots. Problems of all shapes and sizes can also be noted and addressed through video surveillance. For example, imagine a video camera installed in a local town square. Reviewing the films, officials might realize that people who meet in the square move quickly into the shade of the one tree in the center of the square. This could move officials to plant more trees or provide tables with umbrellas so that people could meet and relax in the shade. Similarly, a video camera in a grocery store might reveal that Isle 7 is always overcrowded, prompting the manager to re-arrange items to more evenly distribute shoppers.

Of course it's possible to have too much of a good thing, and if surveillance cameras cross the line and start being installed on private property— that is, in our offices and homes—then we will have the "Big Brother is watching" scenario opponents fear. If that were the case, I would be against surveillance cameras, too. But as long as surveillance cameras are limited to public places, they can help ensure our safety.

Sample 4 Score

Many public places now have surveillance cameras, the main reason being to ensure safety. I think this is a good idea, and that more places should have them.

Surveillance cameras are a good thing because they help keep us safe. If people know they might be on video then, they probably won't do something bad or against the law, like stealing. This is a big protection for us. It makes me feel safer, especially like in a parking lot in the night time. The other good thing about surveillance cameras, is that they can help us catch someone who does do something bad. For example, stealing a car in a parking lot. The camera can get a good picture of the thief and the police will have a good description of the person who stole the car. That makes it a lot easier to catch the thief.

I think surveillance cameras can also be used for other good things, like helping fix traffic jams in grocery stores. I mean if you can see that people are always crowding in one isle, for example.

I know that some people are upset about this kind of thing (being on film) and think that it's like "Big Brother is watching," or something. Also, some people just don't like being on cameras. However, if you're not doing anything wrong, it shouldn't matter. Their only for finding people who do things wrong. To me, I think that makes a lot of sense.

Sample 1 Score

In my opinion, should we install more surveillance cameras in public places? I think, "yes," is a good idea. Why or why not? In my opinion, it is for making ensured the safety in places such as parking lots. This is what our right to privacy can do and tell the law enforcement officials and government too.

95. Alexander Smith said, "The great man is the man who does a thing for the first time." Do you agree with this definition of greatness? Why or why not?

Sample 6 Score

Just as there are many definitions of success, there are also many definitions of greatness. Alexander Smith said that a great person is someone who does a thing for the first time. He's right, and the list of those great people is long and includes the likes of Neil Armstrong, Jackie Robinson, and Thomas Edison. But Smith's definition isn't broad enough to include many other people who I believe are also great. In my opinion, greatness can also be attained by doing something to improve the lives of others.

Mother Teresa is the first person to come to mind under this broadened definition. Mother Teresa, who received the Nobel Peace Prize in 1979, dedicated her life to helping the poor, the sick, and the hungry. She left her homeland of Yugoslavia to work with the impoverished people of India, where she selflessly served others for almost 70 years. She became a nun and founded the Missionaries of Charity sisterhood and the House for the Dying. She embraced those that many in society chose to disdain and ignore: the crippled and diseased, the homeless and helpless. She gave them food, shelter, medical care, and the compassion that so many others denied them. She was certainly not the first to dedicate her life to the care of others, but she was certainly a great woman.

Another great person who also won a Nobel Peace Prize was Dr. Albert Schweitzer, a German doctor who, like Mother Teresa, also selflessly served the poor and sick. Schweitzer dedicated himself to the people of Africa. There, he built a hospital and a leper colony, a refuge for those who had been rejected by society. Again, he was not the first to offer care and comfort for the sick and suffering. But he certainly was great.

Harriet Tubman is also clearly a great woman. She led hundreds of American slaves to freedom along the underground railroad, risking her life over and over again to bring her fellow slaves to freedom. She gave them the greatest gift one can offer: freedom to live a better way of life. She wasn't the first to escape, and she wasn't the first to go back for others. But she was the one who kept going back. She knew that each time she returned for another, she was risking her life. But like Mother Teresa and Dr. Schweitzer, Harriet Tubman was utterly dedicated to improving the life of others.

Greatness comes in many forms, and we are lucky to have many examples of greatness upon which to model our lives. Some great people are those who were able to be the first to accomplish something marvelous. Others, like Mother Teresa, Albert Schweitzer, and Harriet Tubman, are great because they worked tirelessly to ease the suffering of their fellow human beings.

Sample 4 Score

According to Alexander Smith, "The great man is the man who does a thing for the first time." In my opinion, this is a good definition, but it is also too narrow. By that I mean that it is not broad enough to include lots of other people that I believe are great. There are many people who didn't necessarily do anything for the first time who have done great things.

One example was Mother Teresa. Another is Albert Schweitzer, and a third is Harriet Tubman.

Albert Schweitzer opened up a hospital and leper colony in Africa to take care of the sick and abandoned people who had no money or access to health care. This was a great thing. Without his hospital, people would die or suffer and be outcast by society.

Harriet Tubman is famous for being a woman who kept going back to the South to free slaves. She led them through the "underground railroad" and brought them to freedom. She wasn't the first to escape or help others escape, but she was great because she kept doing it and kept helping others.

Finally, Mother Teresa helped so many people. She went to India and opened up a place for the sick and the dying to be taken care of. She helped to feed and comfort hungry and sick people, thousands of them. She is what it means, to be compassionate towards others.

All three of these people and lots of others like them are great for what they did to help others.

Sample 1 Score

What does it mean, to be great. Alexander Smith say that "The great man is the man who does a thing for the first time." I know a lot of great men, the list can be long: George Washington, Robert Kennedy, Mother Teresa, Harriet Tubman, Beethoven, Jackie Robinson, Reggie Jackson (I like baseball), Martin Luther King, and etc. the list goes on and on.

To be great is not an easy thing. Having to do something for the first time, or doing something else that is great. You can be leading others or helping them. In fact not everyone who does this is great.

107. Should people lease or buy new cars? Make a case for the option that you think is best. Use specific reasons and examples to support your position.

Sample 6 Score

Planning to lease a car because you don't think you can afford to buy? Think again. Leasing can end up being just as expensive as buying—and you don't even get to keep the car. Even if you decide to buy the car at the end of your lease, you may end up paying considerably more money than if you'd decided to buy from the beginning.

Most people who are thinking about leasing are attracted to this option because they believe it will cost them less money. And they're right—it is cheaper, but only in the short term. For example, if you were to lease a 2002 Subaru Forester, with $2,500 down, you might pay $250 per month for the car. If you were to buy the same car, with $2,500 down, you would pay closer to $350 per month. Over a three-year lease, that's $3,600—a big savings. But after your lease is over, you have to give the car back. If you want to keep driving, you'll either have to put another down-payment on another lease, or, if you have the option to buy the car, you'll have to pay thousands of dollars to purchase the vehicle—dollars that won't be spread out in more manageable monthly payments.

Many people want to lease because they can then drive a nicer car than they might otherwise be able to afford. For example, if your monthly budget allowed you to spend $250 on your car, you might be able to lease a brand new Ford Explorer. For the same price, you might have to buy an Explorer that was two or three years old with 50,000 miles, or buy a new but considerably less expensive make and model. A lease therefore allows you to drive in the latest models of more expensive cars. But when your lease is over, you will have to return that Explorer. Whatever car you can afford to buy, you get to keep it, and it will always have a resell or trade-in value if you wanted to later upgrade to a newer car.

Furthermore, people who lease cars are often shocked by how much they must pay when the lease is over. Most leases limit you to a certain number of miles, and if you go over that allotment, you must pay for each mile. As a result, at the end of your lease, you may end up paying thousands of dollars in mileage fees. For example, if your lease covers you for 25,000 miles over three years, but you drive 40,000, that's an extra 15,000 miles. At $.11 per mile, that's $1,650 you'll have to pay. And you still won't have a car.

In addition, when you lease, you still have to pay for regular maintenance and repairs to the vehicle. Since you must return the car when your lease expires, you are paying to repair *someone else's car.* If you own the car, however, you would know that every dollar you spend maintaining or repairing the car is an investment in a real piece of property—your property, not someone else's.

By now, the benefits of buying over leasing should be clear. But if you're still not convinced, remember this fundamental fact: If you lease, when your lease is up, after you've made all of your monthly payments, paid for extra mileage, and paid for repairs, *you must give the car back.* It isn't yours to keep, no matter how much the lease cost you. Whatever make or model you can afford to buy, it is yours to keep after you make your payments. There's no giving it back, and that makes all the difference.

Sample 4 Score

When you need a car, you can lease, or buy it. A lot of people think leasing is better, than buying. I think it makes more sense to buy. It really actually costs less money in the long run.

With a lease you can pay less each month for a car. If you buy it you'd probably have to pay a lot more each month, like a hundred dollars more a month. But the good thing about buying is you get to keep the car. With a lease of course, you have to give the car back.

With a lease you also have to pay for the extra miles you put on the car.

You are only allowed to put so many miles on the car and if you go over that, you have to pay for each mile. That can add up to thousands of dollars even though its only a few sense for each mile.

You will also need to pay for any repairs on the car just like you would if you owned it, which you don't, because you still have to give it back. When you owne the car, you still have to pay for repairs, but, it's your car. Leasing feels like throwing money away.

Sample 1 Score

Lot of people they buy car, so many others they leasing. Leasing mean pay money each month and then giving the car back. Leasing can be for one year or two even three or four. Most any car, you can lease it. Any car you can buy, too, new one or use one.

Leasing sometime you pay fewer monies because you don't keep the car. Buying sometime it cost more but you keep the car. Down paying can be a lot of money and hard to save.

Buying or leasing, is up to you. Which works for you.

108. The inventor and statesman Benjamin Franklin said, "Money never made a man happy yet, nor will it. There is nothing in its nature to produce happiness." Do you agree with this statement? Why or why not? Use specific reasons and examples to support your position.

Sample 6 Score

Benjamin Franklin is one of the greatest figures in American history, and I have a great deal of respect for this incredible inventor, politician, and writer. But I must respectfully disagree with his claim that, "Money never made a man happy yet, nor will it. There is nothing in its nature to produce happiness." I agree that money in and of itself does not make a person happy; but I believe that money can help provide one thing that is essential to happiness: good health.

While money can do nothing to change our genetic makeup and our physiological predisposition to illness and disease, it *can* give us access to better healthcare throughout our lives. This begins with prenatal care and childhood vaccinations. In impoverished third-world countries, infant mortality rates are three, four, even ten times higher than in the United States, and as many as one in four women still die in childbirth because they do not have access to modern medical care. Sadly, people who are too poor to afford vaccinations and routine healthcare for their children watch help-lessly as many of those children succumb to illnesses and diseases that are rarely fatal here in the United States.

Money also enables us to afford better doctors and see specialists throughout our lives. If your child has difficulty hearing, for example, and you have insurance (which costs money) or cash, you can see a hearing spe-cialist and pay for therapy. If you have migraines that make you miserable, you can see a headache specialist and afford medication and treatment. Hav-ing money also means being able to afford preventative measures, such as taking vitamins and getting regular check-ups. It means being able to afford products and services that can enhance our health, such as gym member-ships, organic foods, and acupuncture.

Another important thing money can do is enable us to live in a healthy environment. Many of the world's poorest people live in dirty, dangerous places—unsanitary slums crawling with diseases and health hazards of all sorts. In a particularly poor area of the Bronx, for example, children had an abnormally high rate of asthma because their families couldn't afford to move away from the medical waste treatment plant that was poisoning the air.

Money can also help us be healthy by enabling us to afford proper heat-ing and cooling measures. This includes being able to afford a warm win-ter coat and the opportunity to cool off at a pool or in the ocean. On a more basic level, it means being able to afford heat in the winter and air condi-tioning in the summer. During heat waves, victims of heat stroke are often those who are too poor to afford air conditioning in their apartments. In extreme cold, the same is true: people who freeze to death or become gravely ill from the cold are often those who are unable to afford high heat-ing bills.

Having money may not make people happy, but it sure goes a long way toward keeping them healthy. And as they say, if you haven't got your health, you haven't got anything.

Sample 4 Score

Benjamin Franklin once said that "Money never made a man happy yet, nor will it. There is nothing in its nature to produce happiness." I do not agree with this statement because money can buy access to good health care. In my opinion, good health is essential to happiness. Therefore, money can make you happy by keeping you healthy.

Money first of all can get you access to good doctors, even specialists if you need them. With money, you can afford all kinds of things, like tests that check for diseases and special treatments if you find something wrong. If your pregnant you can get good pre-natal care and have a good birth, while in poor countries lots of women die in childbirth and lots of babies die while their infants.

If you have money you can buy an air conditioner so it's not too hot in the summer and you can afford to have heat all winter. If you don't you might suffocate in the heat or freeze to death. You can also stay out of poor areas like slums which are unhealthy and dangerous to live in.

As they say, money can't buy you love, but I think it can buy you good health, and if you don't feel good, it's hard to be happy.

Sample 1 Score

Benjamin Franklin was a great inventer of America. He famous for inventing electricity. He also wrote a lot. One thing he said once was that "Money never made a man happy yet, nor will it. There is nothing in its nature to produce happiness." Do you agree or disagree with this statement? Every one has their opinion. Another question is what is happiness? I also like to be with my family and friends.

Some times I need money to spend with them, like to fly on a plane to see my brother in Colorado. It is as beautifol there as every one told me it was.

109. Some states have now made it illegal to drive while talking on a hand-held cellular phone. Do you think this is a good law that should be passed in other states as well? Why or why not? Explain your answer.

Sample 6 Score

No matter how careful a driver you may be, when you do something else while driving, whether it's drinking coffee, changing the radio station, looking at a map, or making a call on your cell phone, you endanger yourself and others because you are distracted from your driving. Even a fraction of a second of distraction is enough to cause an accident. While no state can make it illegal to drink coffee or switch stations while driving, all states can, and should, make it illegal to drive while talking on a cellular phone.

In the past decade, as the popularity of cellular phones has risen, so have the number of accidents caused by people talking on their cell phones. Whether they were dialing a number, listening to a message, or simply in a heated conversation, they were momentarily distracted from the task of driving, and suddenly—*crash!* Fortunately, many of these accidents have been minor fender-benders. But all too many have been deadly accidents that could have been prevented by a stricter cell-phone use laws.

Cell phone proponents may argue that talking on a cell phone is no more dangerous than, for example, having a cup of coffee while on the road or talking to someone in the back seat. But unlike a cup of coffee, which you can put down between sips, you must keep the phone in your hand. That means that you have only one hand on the wheel while you're driving. That makes cell phones doubly dangerous: not only are you distracted by dialing or by the conversation; you are also driving one-handed, which means you are less in control. If you suddenly need both hands on the wheel to prevent an accident or to keep your car from sliding, the extra second it takes to get your hand back on the wheel can make the difference between an accident and an accident narrowly averted, between a serious injury and a minor one.

Cell phones are also dangerous because when you are busy talking, especially if you really have to concentrate on the matter you are discussing, your mind is not fully focused on the road, and this has a significant effect on your reaction time. You will be slower to make important driving decisions such as how soon to brake and when to switch lanes, and you will be less able to respond to situations on the road.

Many people use cell phones to report accidents and emergencies, to let loved ones know they'll be late, and to stay in touch when they're out of town. I'm not arguing that you shouldn't have a cell phone in your car. What I am saying is that you shouldn't be driving when you're talking on that phone. Until your state outlaws hand-held cell phones in cars, pull over to the side of the road when you are ready to make a call. It may add a few extra minutes to your commute, but it just might save your life.

Sample 4 Score

Driving with a cell phone is dangerous, and it should be illegal. Its all ready illegal in some states, in my opinion it, should be illegal in all of them.

First of all, driving with a cell phone is dangerous because your distracted. Especially when you're dialing a number, then you're not even looking at the road. What if the cars in front of you suddenly stop?

You can also be distracted by the conversation you are having and lose focus from driving. This means that you may not be able to react quick enough to dangers on the road. Another problem is that with a cell phone, you don't have both hands on the wheel, and that's for the whole time you're talking. You can't make sharp turns and handle sudden curves with just one hand.

Lots of people think, oh, it's just one quick call, no problem. But even just a quick call makes you distracted, even just for a quick second. That's enough to cause an accident. So don't drive when you need to talk on your cell phone. Instead, be safe and pull over.

Sample 1 Score

In many states of the United States they make it again the law for talking while driving with cellular telephone. In my opinion, is this a good idea? I believe.

For to many accidents, are happening with the cellular telephone, the driver he don't see (what happens) ahead. This terrible for every one especial the ones they getting hurt. Some accident really very terrible and, everyone going to the hospital. This should be the law.

Expository Writing Prompts

Choose one of the expository writing prompts from the list below and write an essay. A certain number of prompts have model essays in the answer section that you can use to compare and contrast your writing. A scoring guide or rubric is also included in the answer section. You can use this guide to give you an idea of the way your essay may be graded. If you have trouble interpreting the scoring guide, see a teacher or professor for help. Sample responses to the prompts in bold can be found at the end of the section.

126. Explain outdoor living to a person with an apartment in the city.

127. Explain how two people of different interests and backgrounds could become unlikely allies.

128. Describe a family celebration that has special meaning for you.

129. Tell about a world-class athlete. Explain why you include this person in that category.

130. Explain the problems, both personal and societal, that result from obesity.

131. Describe your vision of an ideal vacation.

132. Explain, in detail, a situation where a change of plans becomes necessary.

133. **Describe the purposes of the Internet. Include various viewpoints, including that of users and providers.**

134. Describe how and why people choose the particular foods they eat.

135. **Describe various styles of shoes as well as reasons for their popularity.**

136. **Math is a required subject. Explain why it is so important.**

137. Discuss the causes of and problems resulting from teenage smoking.

138. Discuss a public health concern that you believe is serious enough to warrant immediate attention.

139. **Describe a major environmental problem and what you believe should be done about it.**

140. Discuss how a person achieves fame and fortune and how it changes the individual's life.

141. Discuss how conveniences change people's lives.

142. Describe techniques or methods that could help teachers do their job more effectively.

143. **Describe how communication has changed in the last 20 years.**

144. Describe, in detail, a team sport that interests you.

145. Explain why a particular adjective describes you perfectly.

146. Explain what cooperation means to you and why it is important.

147. Explain the meaning of diversity.

148. Discuss the importance of pride in one's work.

149. What is special about you? Explain what makes you a unique individual.

150. Discuss the events in the life of your favorite author, sports figure, or performer. Explain how these events relate to the person's achievements.

151. Describe techniques and behavior that make a person a good driver.

152. Explain why some people may be afraid of sharks.

153. Explain how different modern life would be without computers.

154. Explain pollution to a visitor from another planet.

155. Explain to a doctor what would be helpful during an office visit.

156. Explain the causes and effects of a poor diet.

157. Explain the causes and effects of impulse buying.

158. Explain the causes and effects of not voting in elections.

159. Explain the causes and effects of prejudice.

160. Describe how to be a good citizen.

161. Describe your favorite game. Explain why it is your favorite.

162. Tell how to pack for a camping trip.

163. Describe how weather affects your commute to school.

164. Tell how you can make a new friend.

165. Explain what you should do if you want to end a relationship.

166. Explain some of the best ways to prepare for a job interview.

167. Explain how to have a winning baseball team.

168. You must pass a college admissions test. Explain what you have to do to achieve this goal.

169. You want to buy a new state of the art computer. Detail the steps you would have to take to ensure that you will make an appropriate decision regarding this major investment.

170. Brothers and sisters do not always get along. Describe the kinds of problems this discord creates in families and the best way to handle a situation like this.

171. Explain how to pick the best candidate for an elected office.

172. Describe your favorite season and explain why it is your favorite.

173. Describe a vegetable that you truly dislike.

174. Describe a typical day of your life.

175. Explain what you might do to help a sick friend or relative.

176. Describe how to brush your teeth.

177. Describe how a person should choose a new outfit.

178. Explain how to choose a pet that matches your lifestyle.

179. You decide to write a mystery. Describe the steps you would take to write a bestseller.

180. Explain how you should read a book to a child.

181. Explain how to set a table for company.

182. Explain how to become a smart consumer.

183. Explain how to write a good resume.

184. Describe a master plan that would make your community a better place to live.

185. Describe your school.

186. Describe how to build a birdhouse.

187. Describe how to paint a room.

188. Explain how you would find a good restaurant in a place you are visiting for the first time.

189. Explain to a person who has a great many debts about life on a budget.

190. Describe the chores and responsibilities that you have at home.

191. Describe what you can do to save money and still cover your basic needs.

192. Explain how to choose the right college.

193. Explain what you would do if you won the lottery.

194. Describe the steps you would take if you wanted to research your family tree.

195. With the hope of preserving family history, describe the kinds of questions to ask an older relative.

196. You are asked to write an article about a person newly arrived from another country. Discuss the kinds of information you would include.

197. Describe how manners have changed over time.

198. Discuss reasons for appreciating your parents.

199. Describe how to show appreciation to your parents.

200. If you could live in any decade, which one would you choose and why?

201. Describe how to perform your favorite magic trick.

202. Your best friend's birthday is coming up. Describe the plan you created to make this birthday celebration the kind your friend will always remember.

203. Describe the steps you will take to launch a new career.

204. Describe how you would decorate a dorm room, living room, or office.

205. Describe the tasks you need to complete before you attend college in another state.

206. **Your new job requires that you move to a different city. Describe the steps you will take to prepare for this move.**

207. Choose a foreign country you would like to visit and explain why you find that country so appealing.

208. Describe how climate dictates lifestyle.

209. Tell how customers like to be treated in a store.

210. Explain how different modern life would be without phones.

211. Describe the menu for a satisfying dinner in a restaurant.

212. Describe the menu and setting of a romantic dinner for two.

213. Describe the perfect menu for a picnic at the beach.

214. Describe the most luscious, decadent dessert you can imagine.

215. Tell how you would entertain a group of five-year-olds on a rainy afternoon.

216. Give someone directions from your school to your house.

217. Many people spend a great deal of time with animals. Write about the relationships that people have with animals.

218. Tell how you can protect your house from intruders.

219. Describe the best way to honor a hero.

220. You are asked to landscape the front yard of a new house. Describe the steps you would take from the beginning of the process to its completion.

221. Describe a teenage fad and the reasons you believe caused its popularity.

222. Describe a favorite music video to a friend who has not had a chance to see or hear it.

223. You are about to spend a year abroad and must learn a new language. Describe the steps you would take to accomplish this goal as quickly as possible.

224. Describe a favorite movie to a person who wants to know all about it but will not have the opportunity to see it.

225. Explain how not getting enough sleep affects your day.

226. Describe the most effective teacher you have ever had.

227. Describe a person who is especially interesting.

228. **Describe an especially memorable photo or picture.**

229. Compare and contrast 1900 with Y2K.

230. Compare and contrast two strategic sport plays.

231. Compare and contrast checkers and chess.

232. Compare and contrast understanding and knowledge.

233. Compare and contrast a screen actor with a stage actor.

234. Compare and contrast any two U.S. presidents.

235. Compare and contrast a budget and an allowance.

236. Compare and contrast public schooling and homeschooling.

237. Compare and contrast learning and teaching.

238. Describe how weather affects your mood.

239. Compare and contrast a vacation in a cold climate and a vacation in a warm climate.

240. Compare and contrast spicy foods and sweet foods.

241. Compare and contrast foods you eat raw and foods that are cooked.

242. Compare and contrast dressing for a formal occasion and dressing informally.

243. Compare and contrast cats and dogs.

244. Compare and contrast microscopes and telescopes.

245. Compare and contrast whales and sharks.

246. Write a letter to a teacher requesting information about a poor grade.

247. You want to organize a family reunion. Describe the steps you will take to contact people and to organize the event.

248. Write an e-mail message to your colleagues, inviting them to a Memorial Day celebration.

249. Write an e-mail message to a company complaining about a defective product.

250. Describe a four-hour bicycle trip through mountainous terrain.

RUBRIC FOR EXPOSITORY WRITING

Score	6	5	4	3	2	1
	For a grade at this level, your writing:	For a grade at this level, your writing:	For a grade at this level, your writing:	For a grade at this level, your writing:	For a grade at this level, your writing:	For a grade at this level, your writing:
Content: Your written response shows an understanding and interpretation of the writing prompt.	▪ satisfies the requirements of the writing prompt in a creative and original manner. ▪ uses an obvious theme throughout.	▪ provides a thoughtful analysis of the writing prompt. ▪ uses a clear theme throughout.	▪ meets some of the requirements of the writing prompt. ▪ includes some key elements that help explain the thesis.	▪ offers a simple interpretation of the writing prompt. ▪ lacks a theme.	▪ meets few of the requirements of the writing prompt. ▪ discusses very basic ideas. ▪ makes few connections to help explain the thesis.	▪ minimally addresses the writing prompt. ▪ digresses, repeats, or dwells on insignificant details throughout.
Development: Your written response gives a clear and logical explanation of ideas, using supporting material.	▪ builds and elaborates ideas thoroughly. ▪ uses examples precisely. ▪ develops the topic in an interesting and imaginative way. ▪ demonstrates coherence in the development of ideas.	▪ develops the topic in an acceptable way. ▪ uses relevant examples throughout the essay. ▪ develops ideas clearly and consistently.	▪ answers the question in an abbreviated manner. ▪ gives brief examples to explain ideas. ▪ develops ideas somewhat inconsistently.	▪ shows weakness in development of ideas and/or develops ideas without thorough explanation.	▪ contains inaccurate, vague, or repetitive details. ▪ has limited development of ideas.	▪ shows a lack of development of ideas.
Organization: Your written response shows a coherent, orderly, well-reasoned approach.	▪ sets up and maintains a clear focus. ▪ establishes a logical, rational sequence of ideas with transitional words and sentences.	▪ has an obvious plan of organization. ▪ focuses on the thesis statement. ▪ uses appropriate devices and transitions.	▪ has a general focus. ▪ obviously attempts organization. ▪ exhibits a logical sequence of ideas.	▪ does not show a logical sense of organization. ▪ strays from the topic. ▪ can be difficult to follow.	▪ shows an attempt to create a focus. ▪ digresses from the topic. ▪ is disorganized.	▪ is less organized than a 2-point response. ▪ exhibits no organizational pattern or focus.
Conventions/ Language Use: Your written response shows a sense of audience by using effective vocabulary and varied sentence structure.	▪ has vivid language, fluidity, and a sense of engagement and voice. ▪ has sophisticated style of sentence structure, sentence variety, and vocabulary. ▪ has essentially no errors.	▪ has good control of mechanics. ▪ contains some errors when using sophisticated language. ▪ has a slightly lower quality of sentence structure and sentence variety. ▪ shows errors when using sophisticated vocabulary only.	▪ has a sense of audience. ▪ uses simple sentences. ▪ uses an appropriate level of vocabulary. ▪ demonstrates partial control of mechanics. ▪ exhibits some errors that do not interfere with comprehension.	▪ uses vocabulary that is slightly below level. ▪ has a vague sense of audience. ▪ shows a beginner's control of the language. ▪ has errors that begin to interfere with comprehension.	▪ exhibits little control of the language. ▪ has errors that make comprehension difficult.	▪ shows minimal control of language skills. ▪ may be illegible or unrecognizable as English.

A ZERO PAPER is:
▪ totally unrelated to the topic.
▪ filled with indecipherable words and is illegible.
▪ incoherent with illogical or garbled syntax.
▪ blank.

Scoring Explanations for Expository Writing Essays

A score of "**6**" indicates that your essay satisfies the requirements of the writing prompt in a creative and original manner, using an obvious theme and thesis throughout. Your essay provides a clear and logical explanation and uses support material. Your ideas are articulated in a coherent fashion; there are precise examples; and the topic is developed in an interesting manner. Your essay is well reasoned, with a clear focus, a logical sequence of ideas, and transitional words and sentences. You demonstrate a sense of audience by using effective vocabulary, varied sentence structure, and fluid, sophisticated language that is essentially without errors.

A score of "**4**" indicates that your essay meets some of the requirements of the writing prompt, including some key elements that help explain the thesis. Your essay may answer the question in an abbreviated manner, giving only brief examples and developing ideas somewhat inconsistently. Your essay has a general focus, makes an obvious attempt at organization, and presents ideas in a logical sequence. The language of your essay indicates a general control of mechanics but has a slightly lower quality of sentence structure and variety than a sample 6 score. An essay of this type contains errors only when using sophisticated language.

A score of "**1**" indicates that the essay only minimally addresses the writing prompt, digressing, repeating, or dwelling on insignificant details throughout. The essay shows a lack of development and exhibits no organizational pattern or focus. Your language skills may be illegible or unrecognizable as English.

Model Expository Writing Essays

130. Explain the problems, both personal and societal, that result from obesity.

Sample 6 Score

A single overweight person might not warrant much attention. But a nation whose population is increasingly obese is cause for concern. In the United States, 14% of children and teenagers are categorized as overweight. Why is this a serious problem instead of simply a matter of personal choice? What are the causes of this constantly increasing percentage of obese persons? What is to be done about this, and what organized steps should be taken to solve the problem?

Just as there are ripples from a stone thrown into the water, there are far-reaching and unending effects resulting from obesity. From a psychological perspective, most obese persons would prefer not to be overweight. Our society glorifies the ultra-thin, so if you are obese you do not fit in with acceptable modes of appearance. We know that children are often cruel about taunting their heavy classmates. All too often we hear friends say, "I've got to lose weight before that trip," or "before the wedding." However, there are more objective measures of the negative results of obesity. Type 2 (adult onset) diabetes, an illness with serious consequences, including damage to the heart, damage to the eyes and difficulty in healing infections is attributed to obesity. Public health agencies are dealing with the continual rise in this type of diabetes. Asthma is also on the rise as a result of the obesity epidemic as are sleep disorders such as sleep apnea. Recent research indicates a relationship between some types of cancer and obesity. Society pays the price when citizens are ill, are unable to work, and require constant medical care.

Questions arise: "What can be done about this?" "Who or what is to blame?" Discussing blame is a delicate problem. There are undoubtedly overweight individuals with inherited tendencies toward diabetes or heart disease, and there is evidence that a hormone that gives people a sense of fullness after eating may be lacking in some obese people. Yet, knowing that they are at risk would suggest that steps be taken to thwart the onset of the physical consequences of obesity.

Most authorities agree that diet is key. The avoidance of foods high in sugars, carbohydrates, and saturated fats is recommended by most physicians as a way to ward off obesity and its dire consequences. But this is difficult in our society where fast food outlets are ubiquitous, where we are bombarded by advertising of unhealthy foods, and where we lead increasingly sedentary lives. Sugar-laden soft drinks are sold in schools and profits from these sales are high. An elementary school in Los Angeles received $50,000 for allowing Coca-Cola to install its vending machines. This company and Pepsico constitute the majority of the school soft drink market, and while they profit from the present sales, they are also building brand loyalty and creating future habitual soft drink consumers.

Lack of adequate exercise is a concomitant contributor to the rise in obesity. Children are often playing video games instead of engaging in sports. Adults watch television instead of exercising. People will drive around shopping centers to avoid walking a few extra steps. The quintessential "couch potato" invention has just been invented. Now you can get a universal remote with which, from your comfortable couch, you can not only control your television, but your oven, lights and, presumably, other things which we can only begin to imagine.

Society suffers when its population is increasingly unhealthy, has rising medical costs, notes absenteeism from work and school, and has social inequalities. This latter result, social inequalities, reflects the assertion recently made by a school administrator that 50% of children in poorer school districts are obese. Experts seem to believe that obesity is a problem that can, with diligence and desire, be eliminated or at least mitigated with two simple changes in lifestyle—eating more healthily and getting more exercise.

Sample 4 Score

Obesity is a growing problem in this country. But I don't think obese people actually want to be overweight because being overweight makes you get sick more often. Doctors say obesity causes asma, diabetes, and even heart disease. If people understood the effects of obesity, they would probably try harder to lose weight because no one likes to get sick. Being sick makes kids miss school and adults miss work and often causes a lot of hospital bills. So, in the end, obesity hurts kids educations and their parent's jobs and is also incredibly expensive.

Lately, more and more kids are becoming obese. This is a real problem because teenagers shouldn't have to worry about their heart! They should be playing sports and having fun and getting an education. But when students have asma attacks, they can't breath, which means they can't go to class or take gym. So, having asma and missing school interferes with their education.

Obesity also causes diabetes, a really terrible disease that can make you blind. Of course, some people get diabetes because their parents have it not because they're obese. Heart disease is the number one cause of death in America and can also be caused by obesity. In a way, obesity is more than just being overweight, its like three diseases wrapped up in one. That's exactly why everyone needs to learn more about it, so we can stop it from getting out of hand.

Some people may be obese because they don't like to exercise. But they need to find a way to exercise because if you exercise every day, you will probably stay in shape. Then you won't have to pay expensive doctor bills or go to the hospital as often and everyone will be healthier, miss less school and work, and be better off.

Sample 1 Score

I think obesity is bad but not that bad. If you like sodas you want to have a soda and you may need a mashin. My best friend may be obese but so what if your nice. They try to make you do sports but what if you like tv and the soaps bettr. I don't think yul die if you eat fries and I like that food best so whats the big deel?

133. Describe the purposes of the Internet. Include various viewpoints, including that of users and providers.

Sample 6 Score

In today's world, the first place people turn to when there is a question to be answered, information to be located, or people to be contacted, is often the Internet. Yes, the Internet may have supplanted the traditional encyclopedia as well as a number of other sources of service and information. We can make reservations, plan vacations, play interactive games, learn a language, listen to music or radio programs, read the newspaper, and find out about a medical condition, without coming face to face with another person. There is no limit to the subject matter you can research on the Internet. Just go to a search engine such as Yahoo or Google, type in a few key words or a Web address, and presto, you will probably summon links to more sources than you could have imagined. The Internet allows you to remain at your computer and shop no matter what you wish to purchase. And if you are looking for a bargain or an unusual item, you can go to a popular auction site and either sell or buy.

If, however, you do wish to speak directly to a person, there are the chat rooms. On practically any given topic, groups of people converse with each other. They may be giving opinions about a perfect travel itinerary, a book, or even a political party. The most prevalent use of the Internet also involves directly writing to a person, and that is the sending of e-mail messages to friends and associates. It is possible to communicate instantly with anyone, anywhere, as long as there is an Internet connection. In a world where people frequently travel, where families do not necessarily live in the same neighborhoods, e-mail is a means of making simple, inexpensive, immediate contact. Not only do we send verbal messages, but also now digital cameras take pictures that can be stored and then instantly transmitted on the Internet.

Unfortunately, there are individuals who subvert the opportunities offered by this technology. They are less than honest, disguise their identity, bilk people in financial scams, and entice unsuspecting people, including children, into giving them personal information. Caveats about these problems are currently being publicized so those Internet users will not be victimized.

Of course, the Internet providers, such as AOL, hope to make a profit, and there is usually a monthly fee for the hookup. To increase the profits, the providers sell advertising, which may pop up on the subscriber's screen and require the user to stop and respond, either positively or negatively, to the ads.

When you consider that, among other things, you can hear a concert, read a book, visit a museum and view its contents, visit the websites of numerous individuals and organizations, play a game with one or more people, and pay your bills, you will realize that the uses of the Internet are too vast for a short list. Most would agree that much has been added to peoples' lives by connecting them to the Internet, and that we probably cannot anticipate what new purposes will be explored in the future.

Sample 4 Score

The internet is very useful. You can send e-mail to your friends. They can write back to you. You can do this whenever you want. You can write to people you don't know. You can meet people through the internet. When someone goes to college you can write to them every day.

You can look things up. If you want to find out about something you can look it up. You don't have to go to the library. If you have to read a book you can find out about it and not read it. There are good games you can put in your computer. I like these games. I want to get more games. You can hear good music on the computer. I like to do this. I know how to download the music.

I like to buy stuff on the internet. My friends do this too. I can buy anything and just give a credit card number. I don't have to go the store.

There are many, many things you can do on the internet right from your computer.

Sample 1 Score

I have the internet. I do not use it a lot it takes to long to get things on it if you have to find it out. If you have a computer you shud have it then you can rite on it and music but who nose how the music I like noone els likes I like hard rock what about you.

If you have internet only 1 can use it so how do you no who it is and why fite. If you have a movie more than 1 are alowd not just 1.But the internet has good purposes.

135. Describe various styles of shoes as well as reasons for their popularity.

Sample 6 Score

Visit the shoe department of a large department store and you will undoubtedly see a variety of shoe styles on display. This suggests that the store is satisfying the customers' desire for an assortment of shoes.

Logically, shoes should protect and support the feet. An example of such a shoe is the sneaker. Originally an inexpensive canvas, rubber soled version of a leather oxford (a shoe with laces), the sneaker has become increasing popular and has supplanted the oxford for regular everyday use for many students and some adults. Sneakers, like living things, have evolved and branched out. They are now mostly made of leather and have much cushioning to minimize stress on the wearer's joints. They have become specialized into separate sneakers for walking, running, tennis, and basketball. There are sneakers for aerobic classes, and for the eclectic exerciser, there are cross trainers. There is justification for their popularity for they are comfortable and are engineered to properly support the foot during a particular activity. It has also become acceptable to wear sneakers with street clothes because they just plain feel good. An endorsement by a popular athlete spreads their appeal as well as increases their cost.

At the opposite end of the spectrum is a shoe style that is uncomfortable, harmful, and impractical. These adjectives describe the women's shoes with pointed toes and thin, high heels. Doctors say that the pointed toes cause deformities of the feet, and the three to four inch heels are unstable and can cause back problems. With so many negatives, why are these styles consistently popular? Wearers may admit that they are uncomfortable, but say that they are fashionable and that, in time, they get used to them. Historically, people follow fashion, and here again, advertising preys upon this need to keep up with the current trends.

A shoe that can be totally practical, simply fashionable, or a combination of both, is the boot. For cold or inclement weather, no footwear is as desirable as an insulated, rubber-soled boot. Boots are popular because they are practical, long lasting, and a desirable fashion accessory. But there are boots whose entire function is fashion. Yes, these boots have the same pointed toes and spiked heels as the shoes described above, but they are boots because the leather continues high on the leg.

Historically, shoe styles change, but there are some shoes that are comfortable as well as fashionable, like sandals and sneakers. And, there are those styles some would consider fashionable but harmful to the feet, or worse. If the choice were between comfort or fashion, many people would probably risk discomfort in order to be fashionable.

Sample 4 Score

Shoes are popular because they're necessary for doing almost anything. You need them to walk, play sports, and even to enter drug stores and restaurants. Without them, you'd have to sit at home all day. Shoes also protect your feet when your walking on a hot sidewalk or hiking in the woods. Nowadays, people even use shoes to make fashion statements. Some shoes are more expensive than ever just because they're so popular.

My favorite shoes are my sneakers. Everyone at school has sneakers because they're required for gym class. They're also popular outside of school because they come in so many colors and styles. I have a lot of friends at school but none of us has the exact same pair of sneakers. In high school, sneakers are a good way to express your personality, and on top of that they're really comfortable.

Sandals are also popular, especially in the summer, because they're also comfortable and don't hurt your feet. You can move your toes around when you where them and they don't make your feet sweat like sneakers sometimes do.

I also have new high heel boots with a 4 inch heel. They hurt my feet when I wear them for a long time, but I don't care because they look so cool. I think looking good is worth the pain. Besides, I only wear them on special ocasions. My mother thinks I'll end up ruining my feet, but you should see the heels she wears to work!

Sample 1 Score

I like shoe styles they are good. One time I went to buy shoes and my cuzin was there and we huged becuz we did not see each other for ever. We went to her house and watched tv. I need new sneakers. I like sneakers. They cost to much so I cant get them now. I want high heels my mother wears them and they kill her feet but I want them to. Everyone wants them.

136. Math is a required subject. Explain why it is so important.

Sample 6 Score

If you complain about the universality of math as a required subject, just try and spend one day without encountering some form of mathematics. From page numbers to prices to today's date, math puts things in order and enables us to compare quantitatively. Figuring how much time is required, how much of an ingredient must be measured, how much carpet to buy, all of these everyday experiences require familiarity with math. To survive financially you must use math to allocate your resources. If you want to invest in a business or in the stock market you must know how to deal with the numbers. Understanding graphs and other analyses about the economy or politics or consumer confidence are enhanced by the applications of math. Mathematical applications in the study of science are essential. Tracking the orbits of planets and the locations of stars in the galaxy cannot be done without numerical comparisons. Every discipline, from archeology to zoology, benefits in some way from the use of mathematics.

Practical reasons for the need for mathematics are omnipresent, but there are other, perhaps more esoteric reasons, for interest in this subject. The amazing coincidences found in numbers provide continual fascination. An example is the fact that the sum of the numbers in the products of the "9-times table" add up to nine. Nine times five equals forty-five, and four plus five equals nine. Similarly, the numbers in the product of seven times nine also equal nine. Mathematicians are also especially fascinated with unique geometric relationships. An example is the fact that three pyramids of the same height will exactly fit into a prism of equal height.

A teacher of mathematics once told me, "Math is in everything," and some people say, "Mathematics is the something for which the world was written." These are reasons enough for requiring its study.

Sample 4 Score

Math is a required subject because it is important in school and in every day life. If you don't understand simple math, you'll never know if the cashier is giving you the right change or if your getting a good deal on a new car. Without math, shopping would be impossible. You wouldn't be able to figure out what you could afford. Some people think they don't need math but they do. You need math to know if its hot or cold outside or to know what pages you have to study for a particular test.

Math is also important because you need to use it in almost every other subject. Sometimes you need math in science to make a graph or to measure amounts for an experiment. There's no way you could pass science without math. I use math in history class to remember dates and in English class we use it to understand poetry. You can't even write a haiku without math because you wouldnt be able to count the number of syllables and lines.

In every day life, you need math to balance your checkbook and to know how much time you have before the movie starts. Without it, you'd never be on time, and your friends would hate you. Math is necessary even to make a simple phone call. When you think about it numbers are everywhere so it's important to understand them.

Sample 1 Score
We have to take math. I don't like it. It is stupid. We have to draw in the boxes on graf paper what is this art. I faled art anyway so why do it in math. I can use the kalkuate so I don't even need to study it where allowd to use the kalkuate and so I do not care if math is important.

139. Describe a major environmental problem and what you believe should be done about it.

Sample 6 Score
A major environmental problem, the magnitude of which we are just beginning to realize, is global warming. When people say that the winters aren't as cold as they used to be, or that there was definitely more snow in past years, they are correct. In addition to these personal testimonials, there is concrete visual evidence of global warming. Most noticeable is the depletion of the ice caps. In recent years, glaciers have been receding in greater amounts than in former years. One only has to visit a national park where this recession is marked with signs indicating where the glacier reached in a particular year. The visitor can see how much further away from a particular spot the ice is at the present moment.

When the ice caps, made of fresh water, melt, they change the salinity of the oceans, change the currents, and change the conditions for survival for myriad species. Additionally, invasive species might move in, affecting the entire ecosystem. This has a domino effect, as all species are interdependent and survive according to predictable sources of food and living conditions. A specific example recently described on an environmental calendar told of the effect of global warming on polar bears. The bears cannot go out on the melted ice, which is how they get their food. This causes them to lose body fat and even to be unable to give birth to cubs.

Global warming causes flooding, and because the warming of the earth causes dryness, fires increase.

When speaking of the causes of global warming, some experts say that ice ages followed by warming have been cyclical throughout the eons and that there is not much that can be done about it. However, most scientists believe that the actions of humans have speeded up this process. They blame the increased burning of wood and fossil fuels—oil and coal—on an increasing population needing heat for warmth and cooking. More energy consumption places carbon dioxide and other pollutants in the atmosphere. Warm air trapped around the earth has been deemed the greenhouse effect.

While we cannot stop the naturally occurring climate changes, we can try to mitigate the rapid warming by reducing our use of fossil fuels. Much publicity has been given to the love that Americans have for sports utility vehicles which burn an inordinate amount of fuel and which are not required for the kind of ordinary driving done by most owners. There are numerous additional ways in which we can reduce our dependence on these fuels, ranging from insulating our homes, to lowering the thermostat in winter, and raising it when we use air conditioning. Perhaps researchers can develop alternate sources of energy. Presently an automobile is being developed that uses gas initially and then automatically switches to electricity. Theoretically, this car will be able to run for fifty miles on one gallon of gasoline. Additionally, we can support the scientific study of the effects of global warming. Perhaps we can predict such things as where floods will occur or where crops will have difficulty surviving and take steps to overcome these problems.

One thing is certain. Global warming is a serious environmental problem with ramifications that affect almost every aspect of life.

Sample 4 Score

Global warming which means that it is getting warmer all over the globe, is a serious environmental problem. It is bad for the environment, nature, animals, and humans as well. Global warming causes a lot of glaciers to melt which then causes more floods and makes the ocean warmer which could hurt certain kinds of fish. Global warming also leads to more fires in general and increases the rate of cancer in humans, especially skin cancer.

In order to stop global warming, we should study the greenhouse effect.

Because we use too much oil and gas and pollute the air on a regular basis, hot air can't escape the atmosphere. We need to use less oil and gas so the hot air can get out. People don't need to drive trucks and SUVs all the time because they use more gas and cause more air pollution. We also don't have to use air conditioning all the time. People need to remember that minivans and air conditioning are luxuries not neccessities.

If everyone agreed to change their habits, it would help the environment a lot. So, we should find out what needs to be done to solve this serious environmental problem and do whatever it takes.

Sample 1 Score

A environmental problem is called global warming. The globe is getting hot. I am not sure about this we had plenty of cold days and I like it hot in summr. How do they no do they mesure all over the globe. 1 day it was so cold my hands froze and I got in trubel because I was not aloud out so I had no time to gebt gloves. I gess I don't like global warming if it gets to hot but maybe its only far away anwe don't need to wory about it hear.

143. Describe how communication has changed in the last twenty years.

Sample 6 Score

Who could have predicted twenty years ago that communication would change as radically as it has? Today, communication is instantaneous. No longer do we have to use a pen, pencil, or typewriter to write a letter. No longer do we have to use a postal service to mail it. No longer do we have to wait for a response that takes several days. Nor do we have to stay near a telephone or search for a public phone while traveling. Things have speeded up exponentially.

In the last twenty years we have benefited from tremendous changes in telecommunication. The relatively simple change to portable phones enabled us to roam around the house while chatting, not limited by the length of the cord that attaches the receiver to the base of the telephone. Then came the beeper, allowing us to get a message when away from a telephone. Now, of course, there is the ubiquitous cell phone. Watch the crowds walking along a sidewalk, and you can't help noticing people purposefully striding along while talking on their cell phones.

What if we must write a message? We now have e-mail. We send these messages immediately after typing them on the computer keyboard and never have to go to the Post Office. No more "snail mail." Perhaps we have a written copy that must be sent but cannot be conveniently sent via the computer. Simply dial a phone number, push a few buttons, send a FAX. The copy is transmitted to the receiver at once. The ability to telecommute is almost like handing the copy to the recipient. What a difference twenty years has made. Just as most of us could not imagine the speed and ease of communication in the twenty-first century, we probably cannot anticipate the changes that will occur in the next twenty years. Perhaps we will be able to send instant messages simply by thinking about them, from one brain to the brain of the intended recipient.

Sample 4 Score

I believe communication has definitly changed in the last 20 years. It is much different. I can send e-mails to my friends every day. Even twice a day if I want. I could not do this a few years ago. It's great. So I think communication is much faster and I definitly think it is much easier if you have a computer. Every school and office has a computer.

I believe the best change is the cell phone. I have a cell phone that I carry everywhere I go. I can turn it off in the movie and it will vibrate (shake). Then I know I have a call and I can leave and answer it. I don't think it is right for you to bother someone with your cell phone.

I don't even need stamps to send cards. I can send them on the computer. All my friends have e-mail. And if they don't they don't get a card untill they do.

I can also send a FAX on the telephone if I have to send a copy right then.

These are the ways communication has changed in the last 20 years.

Sample 1 Score

Communication is talking. In some ways it has changed in the last 20 years. I think I can talk easily now because I cary around with my phone. It is pink and everyone likes it. Because I worked to earn it each month. You don't have to read the paper you can watch tv if you want. Tv tells you about clothes and stuff that you care about. So communication is grate. Communication is also the computer which is all over. I hate to rite so I use my cell but I could if I felt like it. My mother uses it. So she says it is much better.

150. Discuss the events in the life of your favorite author, sports figure, or performer. Explain how these events relate to the person's achievements.

Sample 6 Score

Herman Melville was a 19th century writer whose works foreshadowed themes that would become prevalent in the 20th century. He wrote about his distaste for the prevalent oppression of underlings, of the need to accept different cultures and to appreciate the contributions of ordinary people. His novels probe into psychological reasons for characters' actions in a way that would be relevant today.

Born into a New York family that was prominent, although in constant debt, Melville was forced to end his formal schooling at the age of twelve. He was nevertheless widely read and informed on numerous subjects, including, but not limited to, literature, art, science, biology, navigation, mythology, and geography. Thus, he was largely self-educated, as was Ishmael, the narrator of *Moby Dick*, Melville's most acclaimed novel. Ishmael said, "A whale ship was my Yale College and my Harvard."

Just as Ishmael's experiential education mirrored Melville's own informal schooling, so were many other aspects of his life reflected in his writings. Signing up as a cabin boy on a ship going to Liverpool, England, when he was 20, provided Melville with material for the novel, *Redburn*. The novel was about a lonely 20-year old orphan wandering around Liverpool and is thought to be the writer's most autobiographical.

Motivated by the need to earn money, Melville signed up for a four-year voyage as a common seaman in spite of the fact that his family connections could have easily gotten him an officer's commission. Melville had a progressive view about equality that was unusual for his time. He believed in the dignity of all work, which was reflected in his sympathetic, even admiring, excruciatingly detailed, descriptions of the jobs of the working people in his writings. He decried nationalistic prejudice and believed that all people are related. He wrote, "You cannot shed a drop of American blood without shedding blood of the whole world."

Among the first white men to explore the South Sea Islands, Melville was surely the first literary artist to do so. Unable to bear the inhumane treatment on this long voyage, he deserted in the Marquesas Islands. He was ill and fortunately was cared for by a kindly native family. A grown son in the family was covered with tattoos, and Melville learned that these people were cannibals who feasted on their enemies. In order to leave, he had to escape, finding refuge on an Australian ship. He deserted from this ship also, landing in Tahiti. These experiences provided material for the novel *Typee*, about the South Sea Islands, the novel *Omoo*, based upon his experiences in Tahiti, and the novel *White Jacket*, which exposed the cruelty of navy flogging. The tattooed man who cared for Melville provided the prototype for Quequeg, one of the most memorable characters in literature.

Herman Melville also was a crewmember of a whaling voyage where he learned the intricacies involved in this type of multi-year voyage that he used as the setting for *Moby Dick*. This novel, considered a literary masterpiece, provided a forum for Melville's ideas about the necessity for connectedness. The savage, Quequeg, and the sailor, Ishmael, were mutually supportive of this theme. In addition, Melville was a great believer in democracy and the benefits of diversity, and these beliefs were reflected in his descriptions of the crew on the whaling voyage. The ship was a metaphor for the world, with its crew coming from every known location and background, all being necessary for success. A monomaniacal captain, devoid of empathy, driven by his selfish aims, and unable to connect with others, could only lead to disaster.

Thus, Herman Melville's real-life experiences undoubtedly made possible his descriptive novels, but they would not have been possible without his independently drawn conclusions about the dignity of man and his place in the universe.

Sample 4 Score

Herman Melville was a 19th century American writer who wrote many famous books including *Moby Dick*. Like *Moby Dick*, most of his books where about topics that were of personal interest to him like ships and whaling. He spent a lot of time on ships and also knew a lot about whales. Melville led an exciting life and put a lot of that excitement into his books. Because his books were based on real life events and topics he knew alot about, the writing was incredibly detailed and vivid. When people read his books, even when people read them today, they feel as though they've been taken into another world. When you read Melville's books, you learn a lot about whales and foreign lands, but you also learn a lot about him as a person.

Moby Dick is a great book. After reading it, you can understand a lot more about Meville. The story is about a crazy man named Captain Ahab who wants to kill a great whale named Moby Dick. In the book, Melville really seems to care about his characters and makes it clear that all of the characters are equal in his eyes. Ahab's ship is supposed to be a symbol of the entire world and characters like Quequeg and Ishmael are simply every day people. Because Ahab is so selfish, he ends up destroying the entire ship. After realizing that, Melville wants us to know that selfish world leaders will also ruin the world if regular citizens like Ishmael and Quequeg aren't given any power. Melville was all for democracy which you can easily tell after reading this book.

Sample 1 Score

My clas had to read Moby dick. I learned about the author. He is Herman Melville and I like him he is brave he went on trips. I never went on many trips but I wuld. I wuld go to florida. He Herman never went there but he went other places and wrote about it.i don't think nobody in my class akshuly read it.

158. Explain the causes and effects of not voting in elections.

Sample 6 Score

Voting is the privilege for which wars have been fought, protests have been organized, and editorials have been written. "No taxation without representation," was a battle cry of the American Revolution. Women struggled for suffrage as did all minorities. Eighteen year olds clamored for the right to vote, saying that if they were old enough to go to war, they should be allowed to vote. Yet Americans have a deplorable voting history.

Interviewing people about their voting habits is revealing. There are individuals who state, almost boastfully, that they have never voted. They somehow set themselves apart from the requirements of citizenship in a democracy. Many who avoid voting do so consciously. It is not as if they were ill or unavoidably detained on election day. Often they claim that their one vote doesn't matter. "What's one vote?" they ask. Perhaps one vote may not count in some elections, although there have been results determined by one or very few votes. In addition, the total of single votes that are not cast can add up to a significant difference in a particular race. Some people blame the fact that they do not know enough about the issues for their absence from the voting booth. Others say that they avoid learning about the news because it is too depressing. In a democracy, we can express our opinions to our elected leaders, but more than half of us sometimes avoid choosing these people who make the policies that affect our lives.

One of the effects of this statistic is that politicians will cater to the groups that do vote in large numbers, giving more weight to their needs than to those of other groups or of the general population. Since so many do not vote, elected officials can, with impunity, promote policies that benefit the special interests that contribute financially to the election campaigns. Another effect of not voting is the free rein given to those in office to disregard the expressed opinions of constituents. For if you do not vote, why should the candidate worry about you?

It seems ironic that in this most democratic of societies, we abrogate the privilege for which so many have struggled. How many countries do not have a choice of candidates, yet their citizens are forced to participate in sham elections? In the United States we have choices. We can vote to fire an officeholder who does not live up to our expectations by choosing an opponent at the next election, and we are free to choose someone whose ideas appeal to us.

Perhaps a major reason for not voting is the failure to convey how precious and unique is the right to vote and how important is each and every vote. The major effect is that we are voluntarily giving up our rights as citizens to ascertain that our elected officials truly represent us. This is because we have not done our part in choosing them so in effect, we are telling these officials that we don't care enough to bother to vote.

Sample 4 Score

Many people do not vote because they think its a hassle or that their vote won't make a difference. Some people say they don't care who wins, but everyone should care because government officials make decisions that effect all of us. People need to learn more about their own government. So many Americans think our government is made up of one person, the president! But there are so many other people involved and so many other elections to think about too.

Not having time to vote or not knowing who to vote for is no excuse for not voting at all. People should take the time to learn as much as they can about the people who are running and make an informed decision. If you don't vote then you'll never get what you want and you won't be able to complain when politicians make bad decisions.

But if you're smart and vote for whoever you feel is the best candidate, then if that person is elected, you can know that it's their responsibility to listen to you. Our government is supposed to be for the people and run by the people, so everyone should realize it is their right and also their responsbility to vote during every election.

Sample 1 Score

Most people don't vote I wouldn't my mother don't she says she has no time she is so bizy she works and how can she vote if she works. My brother says if you vote you can called to the juree and who need that his friend had it and it was boring and he culdve lost his job. If you care who wins you shud vote if you don't care don't.

167. Explain how to have a winning baseball team.

Sample 6 Score

Whether professional or amateur, a baseball team, like a fine meal, needs the right ingredients to create a winning result. Talented athletes are the first requirement. After that, astute coaching, which discerns and then develops the unique capabilities of the players, can be as important as the athletes themselves. Flexibility and the willingness to try different strategies are the hallmarks of winning coaches. All the talent in the world could be wasted without creative and shrewd coaching.

A player with the ability to sprint, needed both for infield defense and for speedy base running, can be invaluable. A fast runner can steal bases and get to first base with a carefully placed bunt.

Good pitching is essential for a winning baseball team. A pitcher who is "on" is the first line of defense in baseball. It is well known that the pitcher is often the poorest hitter, but it is the pitcher who keeps the opponents from scoring. The pitcher's teammates accept this and acknowledge that it is their job to score the runs. Here again, a good coach decides who is the optimum pitcher for today's game, and equally important, when to take a tired or poorly performing pitcher out of the game.

Recruiting strong and consistent batters will be a factor in creating a winning baseball team. Having a home run hitter with several players who can be counted on to get base hits and pinch hits are needed because the best pitching and the best fielding will be for naught if runs aren't scored.

Even with a plethora of natural ability, to become a winning baseball team, the players must continually practice, not only to maintain their skills, but also to improve them. In fact, a motivated player who practices diligently may eventually surpass those with superior natural ability that is not developed. Along with this desire to continually improve one's individual playing ability, there is the motivation to succeed because of loyalty to the group. This type of *esprit de corps* can make the difference between a good and a winning baseball team. Putting the team first, while striving to give one's all, puts the finishing touches on the recipe for a winning baseball team.

Sample 4 Score

A winning baseball team would need good hitters, fast runners, a skilled pitcher and catcher, and a knowledgable and patient coach. It would also need to have a group of players who got along without any jealousy or hostility and were capable of rooting for each other.

Good hitters and runners are important because you have to get alot of hits and runs to win. You can't win without scoring runs. Also, the runners need to be speedy, so they can get to the base before the ball gets there. You also have to have a skilled pitcher who can strike people out. The pitcher has to be good or else the other team will score more runs and you will lose. The catcher is important as well because if the catcher drops the ball when the pitcher throws it, that is an error.

Finally, you also need to have a good coach who can help the players improve and who knows when to put certain players in the game and when to take them out. The coach should keep the team running smoothly and solve any fights or disagreements.

Sample 1 Score

I don't want to be on a baseball teem but I want to win if I do. My brother did and he never got a hit and he wont even look at me so who cars about baseball. I think you need to be a athleet and take lessons. And I think the uniforms are ugly I don't look good in it and it is swetty. I will pick the best players if I have to play so I mite as well win right.

192. Explain how to choose the right college.

Sample 6 Score

One of the most important decisions young adults make is where to go to school. Your college education will affect the rest of your life, so you should weigh your options carefully. The "perfect" school may not exist, but I believe there are three factors that are integral to choosing the right college: location, size, and curriculum. You can narrow down your search based on these criteria.

First, you should consider location. Some questions you should ask yourself include: Do I prefer to live in a city, the suburbs, or a rural area? Do I want to live in a temperate or colder climate? Do I prefer to be near my family, or in another part of the country? The answers to these questions will help you make the best choice.

Second, you should consider size. Perhaps your high school experience will affect your choice of colleges. If you attended a small high school with a low teacher-student ratio, you may be accustomed to small class sizes and knowing your fellow students extremely well. On the other hand, if you attended a large high school, you may be used to new faces and larger classes. Would you prefer a school such as UCSB with 50,000 students, or a smaller school with fewer than 5,000 students? Remember, the attention you receive will be affected by the size of the student population.

Finally, in order to choose the right college, you should take the time to decide what you would like to study. Although most colleges offer a myriad of courses, some schools specialize in certain fields and subjects or offer a wider selection of classes. For example, if you are interested in studying the Classics, did you know that the University of Texas has one of the best Classics departments in the United States?

Choosing the right college will require some effort. After you have decided the location, size, and curriculum you prefer, do some research. Learn about different colleges from your guidance counselor, the Internet, or from the colleges themselves. As with any important decision, make sure your choice is an educated one.

Sample 4 Score

It's not easy to choose the right college. There are three things you should consider when applying and deciding on a college. These are: location, classes, and size.

First of all, you should decide where you want to go to school for four years. Decide if you want to be in a city or in a rural area, or if you want to be near to or far from your family. Then, if you know what you want to study, you should make sure that the college offers classes. There would be no need to go to a school that does not teach the Classics, if that's what you want to study. Finally, you should think about whether you want to go to a school with alot of students or not too many. For example, there are more than 50,000 students at UCSB, but maybe you prefer to go to a school with only 5,000.

When deciding on a college, take your time and consider all of these things. College is important for the rest of your life so choose wisely!

Sample 1 Score

Evryone shoold go to college because that education are good for You. Its right to go to college becaus you need it for work and job's and life too. The right colege for You is one You like alot when You are done with hi-scool.

206. Your new job requires that you move to a different city. Describe the steps you will take to prepare for this move.

Sample 6 Score

Although Americans move more than most people in the world, a move is acknowledged to be one of life's more stressful experiences. There are, however, steps that can be taken and preparations that can be made which will mitigate the inevitable strain.

If I were to move to a different city because of a job change, I would find a sponsor in the new location, preferably someone who could give me insight into the kind of situation I could expect at the workplace and about the cultural and other differences in the new community. Different cities may be diverse in many ways: in ideas about appropriate behavior, in social expectations, and even in emotional reactions. If the city had special sites or events to generate civic pride, I would like to investigate those. Or there may be popular gathering places such as parks or cafés. This knowledge would be helpful in getting to understand the attitudes of the residents and to become part of the community.

Spending time with a realtor would be a necessity, not only for finding a satisfactory residence, but also for gaining information about different neighborhoods, schools, libraries, and other community resources. In fact, it would be worthwhile to take the time to deliberately explore the community by walking or driving around.

My family members are interested in horses, sailing, and playing bridge. As a way to find out how we can pursue these interests and find people similarly inclined, we could visit stables, marinas, or social clubs. Striking up a conversation with people in these places and telling them that I am moving shortly would create a more knowledgeable transition. In addition to picking the brains of people, there may be published material, such as maps and guidebooks, that could be informative. The same is true of Internet sites.

All this preparation cannot eliminate the probability that leaving my friends, seeing my belongings picked up, packed, and moved to a different city, and facing new routines and new surroundings will be somewhat traumatic. However, visualizing daily life in the new city can help make the move easier and the transition smoother.

Sample 4 Score

If I find out that I have to move to a different city I will try to make some plans. First of all I will have to find a house. I will get a real estate person and look at houses. I will find out how much they cost and if I can afford it. Then I will try to find a nice area. The schools should be good and near the house and the church to.

I like to play basketball and ride my bike and I will look around for places to play. Maybe I can meet some people who live there and make friends. Maybe they can show me around the place. I will try to meet someone who works at the new job. They can give me hints about how things are done there.

I will say goodbye to my friends and give them my new address. It will be sad to move, but also there will be good things coming up. At least I wont be going in cold. I will have a place to live that is nice and I know maybe a few people already. I think I am starting to know what it will be like in my new home.

Sample 1 Score

I have to move becuz my job it changed. I will go there to see what it is there. Is there a good house. I hate to pay for a house they always rip you off and the boss dosent car. I will find our if the boss is good or not like this 1 I hate now. What can you do you want a job rite. I wil sell my house and use it to by the new 1 and I would learn the name of the new city and how to rite it.

217. Many people spend a great deal of time with animals. Write about the relationships that people have with animals.

Sample 6 Score

Since they were first domesticated, people have had relationships with animals that have enhanced their lives. Probably animals that were trained to hunt and to retrieve prey were among the first to become valuable to their owners. Useful animals include those used for transportation, for hauling loads, and, in recent times, to assist handicapped people. The latter are usually dogs trained to guide the blind and to care for paraplegics. Although these animals have specific functions, it is probable that a special bond inevitably arises between them and the humans they serve and this goes far beyond the dependency each has for the other.

Can a relationship with an animal improve a person's health? Many recent reports seem to suggest this possibility. Pets give us abundant and unconditional love. Always happy to see us, our pets allow us to be ourselves, to talk to them, and even to believe that they understand us. When we come home, we might feel reluctant to "talk to ourselves," but it is perfectly all right to greet, chat, and interact with our dog, cat, bird, and even our fish. Some mental health workers are so insistent upon the beneficial influences of pets that they have an animal present during therapy sessions, claiming that this causes patients to be more relaxed and responsive. Studies have proven that relationships with animals reduce stress and actually can measurably lower blood pressure.

For people who are depressed or living alone, having a pet is not only therapeutic; it is a means of encouraging a healthier lifestyle. A pet owner must live according to a regular timetable so that the pet can be fed and cared for appropriately. For dog owners, there is an additional social benefit that accrues from having to go outdoors for a walk. Encountering other dog walkers often leads to further social interaction and, perhaps, friendship. For cat owners, there is the admiration for the cat's characteristic independence, which makes any affection from the cat so much more meaningful. Keeping the bird feeders filled gives a sense of satisfying the needs of creatures that, in turn, delight us with their beauty and their antics.

Other beneficial effects of relationships with animals continue to be discovered. A recent article suggests that kindness to people and animals may be interconnected. Role-playing that increases children's empathy for animals helps them not only psychologically, but also physically and socially. Another discovery shows that riding horses, for reasons not completely understood, has been shown to benefit autistic children. Pet owners can now volunteer to take their pets to hospitals and nursing homes where residents seem to welcome them.

It is probable that continued research will shed additional light on what happens when people and animals form a bond. For the present, it is certain that almost anyone can benefit from the resulting security, understanding, fun, laughter, and love that come from having a pet.

Sample 4 Score

I enjoy my pets. I have a cat and a bird and I like to spend time with them. When no one is home I play with my cat, or I may try to hold my bird. When I have a pet I feel good and happy. Some people have horses for pets. They get to ride them and take care of them. Even if you have a cat and don't have to take it for a walk you have to feed it.

One of the good things about pets is it teaches you things. I learned that I have to take care of my pets. They need me to feed them every day. I think they look at me funny if I forget or if I am late. I no that little babies like to pet animals and that they like them. So there are relationship with animals for all ages. Old people like animals to. If they live alone they can have someone to talk to. Pets are like friends.

I no a blind man and he has a seeing dog and he goes all over with it. So he has a relationship with his dog. The dog helps him and he helps the dog by loving and taking care of it.

Relationships with animals are good for both people and animals.

Sample 1 Score

What are animals that have a relationship they are pets. I have a dog I hate to feed it and it shed but it wags its tale its kut. Wen I got the dog it was little and kut and now it isnt so kut because its to big. But I love it and he loves me not like my boyfreind who I don't have a relationship with. So I have a relationship with my pet it ushuly feel good.

228. Describe an especially memorable photo or picture.

Sample 6 Score

You might think a memorable picture would have vivid color, an appealing or inspirational theme, or be something you might want to display and look at every day. That is not the case with the picture that is most memorable to me. This picture is really a large mural, painted in 1937 by the Spanish artist, Pablo Picasso, to protest the bombing of a small village in northern Spain.

Surprisingly, there is no vivid red color to show the flowing blood. One must imagine this, for the mural is startlingly gray, black, and white. But there is no avoiding the horror of the images. The figures are not realistically drawn, but are cubist and abstract, and it is apparent that innocent civilians are being slaughtered. A mother screams with her mouth wide open, her head tipped back in heart-rending anguish, as she holds her dead baby. A soldier lies dead on the ground, clutching his broken sword, and three other people are shown in shock and agony. Animals, including a tortured horse and a crying bird, are also portrayed as innocent victims of a massacre. Some symbols are open to interpretation. What is the meaning of the bull, which seems simply to be observing, or of the light bulb emitting rays at the top of the mural? Does the bull symbolize brute force, and does the light bulb signify that there is hope? Yet there is no doubt that the distorted, horrible images are intended to shock the viewer. This depiction of human grief is a profound statement of the cruelty and senselessness of war. Limiting the pictures to black and white adds a funereal element to the shocking depiction of the catastrophe.

The memory of the picture cannot be forgotten; it is a metaphor for the senselessness and the horror of war. While it was painted to protest atrocities in a long ago war, it is as relevant today as the recollection of the horrors of September 11th. Perhaps it should be shown to all those who contemplate starting a war. Would it be worth it to have another Guernica?

Sample 4 Score

The picture I remember is Guernica. It is by Picasso. It is not realist. The shapes don't look real but you know what they are in real life. It is in black and white. It is not in color like most pictures. But it really gets to you. It shows people getting killed or already killed. A baby is killed and a soldier is killed. The mother is screaming because her baby is dead. You won't forget that.

What this picture does is to make you know that war kills people and it is just awful. It kills people and it kills animals and even if you are not killed you will probly be screaming or crying. This picture could be for any war it doesn't matter. You remember it because it makes you upset and you wish there would never be a war. Then people wouldn't have to suffer. This picture is memorable because you remember how the people suffered and they probly didn't do anything.

Sample 1 Score

I remember a picture that is very big. It is Guernica. It is about people dieing and screaming and horses. I don't like it it dosent make sens. Who cared about a horse and why is it in black and white. I don't like black and white movies or pithcers. My sister had black and whites at her wedding and of cours I hated it. But I do remember it because everyone is yelling.

246. Write a letter to a teacher requesting information about a poor grade.

Sample 6 Score

Dear Ms. Jones:

Your class was one of the most informative I have ever taken, and I learned a tremendous amount in the relatively short time of one semester. Therefore, I felt obliged to write to you when I received the disappointing grade of "C" on my term paper.

Checking the criteria you provided and thoroughly discussed in class, I felt that I complied with each one in a superior manner, not just passably, as reflected in my grade. Four arguments in support of my thesis were stated and each was in turn discussed with several relevant examples given. You required only three arguments. Bibliographical citations were given in the exact format you demonstrated in class. As suggested, Internet sites were used in addition to first-person accounts and editorial material.

Although I spent an inordinate amount of time on this project , I felt it to be most worthwhile because it was a wonderful learning experience. When I saw the grade on the paper, I looked in vain for comments or suggestions. It would be helpful to me if I understood how you arrived at this grade. Would it be possible for us to arrange a meeting, during which time you could offer hints about what you felt was lacking in my work, and, perhaps, I could hope that you might reconsider and raise my grade.

Thank you for your kind consideration of this request.

Sincerely yours,

Your Student

Sample 4 Score

Dear Ms. Jones:

I was really upset at my grade. I don't think I am a C student. I tried hard and got some B's a few times. Don't you think I did everything on the checklist you gave us? I had the right number of examples and I tried to tell a little about the examples. There was only one where I couldn't get an example, but does that mean I get a C?

I worked hard on this and I think anyone would get a C even if they didn't work so hard. I never did such a long paper. I hope you noticed the good bibliography. I copied it just the way you showed it. And you didn't write any corrections so what was wrong with it?

Could you tell me what was wrong with it. I think I should get at least a B.

Sincerely yours,

Your Student

Sample 1 Score

Dear ms Jones,

Why do you pick on me im as good as anyone. Why do I get the lousy grad. I culdnt do that bibliography but I did do some examples. My friend was over and who had time she was having a big prolben with the famly. I tried to help her but it was no use. Anyway I wish yud be nice for wuns sins its over the class is and whats the big deel. Just give me a better grade I was only abset 8 tims.

Your friend,

A student

247. You want to organize a family reunion. Describe the steps you will take to contact people and to organize the event.

Sample 6 Score

My family is united genetically but not by proximity. We live in far-flung locations, including three continents and both the northern and southern hemispheres. Some of us have kept in touch while others might as well be considered MIA. It would seem close to impossible to organize a family reunion for such a peripatetic group. Yet, that is what I decided to attempt.

Initially I sent e-mails to all those I regularly heard from and requested any and all addresses of other relatives to be forwarded to me. South Africa was the farthest location and was the source of some previously unknown addresses. Internet searches yielded still more. How delighted I was that there seemed to be universal interest in the project. Several people volunteered to help. We generated a list and added to it as soon as we received further information.

Relatives were located in Alaska, Canada, and six states. Thus the first big hurdle was overcome: the list of potential invitees. Then, with solicited input from all concerned, it was decided to choose a location near New York, the original point of origin of the family.

It then became necessary to choose a site for the get-together and then to find accommodations for approximately fifty-five people ranging in age from under one year to eighty-five. An all-suite hotel, which agreed to charge reduced rates if a minimum number of reservations were confirmed was selected. The hotel agreed to hold rooms for us until two weeks prior to the weekend of the get-together. A list of nearby motels and bed and breakfasts was also compiled. We now had the *who*, *where*, and *when*, the latter being the last weekend in September when the weather was still moderate and travel not likely to be a problem. *Why* we were getting together seemed obvious. There was curiosity to catch up, and even to meet relatives known only by reputation.

Now we came to the question of *how* the weekend would be organized. Since most people would be arriving on Friday, that day was to be relaxed and unstructured. On Saturday, there would be games and an informal picnic lunch in a nearby county park, the permission for which was easily obtained. Saturday night would be the highlight, a catered dinner in a restaurant which could easily hold a group of this size. People had been asked to bring photos and anecdotes and a list of speakers was generated. The youngest members would be introduced and those traveling great distances would be recognized. The oldest members might wish to share their reminiscences. Sunday would again be an informal day, probably punctuated with hugs, the sharing of addresses, and promises to do this again. All of the activities would be recorded on videos and a digital camera so that they could easily be forwarded via e-mail. Thus the planning for a family reunion must begin well in advance of the date. Planners must seek out addresses of the relatives, must settle on a location, a date, and, of course, a place to stay. These would vary according to the size and needs of the group. Some groups might prefer to simply chat informally while others would appreciate planned activities. Once a family has done this, a second reunion would be much easier. The addresses are known, faces can be associated with names, and an evaluation of the previous schedule can be solicited. One caveat: have alternate plans in case of bad weather.

Sample 4 Score

The first step in planning a family reunion is having a family. Who is included? Do you invite the divorced ones? After you decide who to invite you should make up a list. Then you should call them, maybe getting someone to help as this is a big job.

The second step is to decide what to do. So you need to know exactly or pretty nearly how many are coming. So you have to pick a date that is good for everyone. Will it be just one day. Or two? You could play games and have people tell stories. It would be fun to hear about things the old people remember. Will you all get together or will it be by ages? You will have to decide. I think it is best to have all ages see each other and become friends if possible.

The third step is deciding where to get together. How about your house?

Do you have room? Do you want the mess? If everyone brings something you will probly still have to get most of the stuff and have the most work anyway. I would do it one time and then have someone else take a turn.

So you now have everybody together for a family reunion. I hope it is fun. I hope it is not boring. I must tell you that some of my known relatives are boring but they are my relatives.

Sample 1 Score

I wanted to try to have a family reunion. My friend had it. What if someone couldn't get there. Well that's life. What if they didn't like the food— hot dogs and hamburgers—well we could ask people to bring something.

One thing I wanted was to see pitchers of my aunt's and uncles and my mom and dad when they were young. Its hard to believe that they were ever kids. Some of the family hates each other at least they don't speak to each other and sometims you cant menshun there names. So what, I can invite them. Acept maybe one dum cousin. But I will take pitchers to show my kids but I don't think I want any. Kids that is.

Narrative Writing Prompts

Choose one of the narrative writing prompts from the list below and write an essay. A certain number of prompts have model essays in the answer section that you can use to compare and contrast your writing. A scoring guide or rubric is also included in the answer section. You can use this guide to give you an idea of the way your essay may be graded. If you have trouble interpreting the scoring guide, see a teacher or professor for help. Sample responses to the prompts in bold can be found at the end of the section.

251. Movies and books often talk about the importance of loyalty and friendship. Tell about a time in your life when friendship proved to be of great importance to you.

252. It is often said that animals are humans' best friends. Describe a time in your life when this saying proved to be true.

253. Martin Luther King, Jr., said that he wished for the day when his children "would be judged not by the color of their skin but by the content of their character." Write about a time in your life when the content of your character was tested.

254. People often say "Don't judge a book by its cover." Describe a time when you misjudged someone based on his or her appearance or when someone misjudged you.

255. The way a person handles disappointment reveals a great deal about what is important to him or her. Tell about a time in your life when you confronted disappointment and how you handled it.

256. As adolescents, many of us promise ourselves that we'll never be like our parents. But as we mature, we often find that we think and act a lot like our parents do. Describe a time when you realized you were behaving like your mother or father (or other guardian) and how that experience helped you better understand your parent.

257. When we reflect upon our childhood, we often come back to a few key events that had a major impact on us. Tell about one of those defining events from your childhood.

258. Sometimes lies can have serious consequences. Describe a time when a lie had major consequences for you.

259. There is a saying that you should be careful what you wish for, because you just might get it. Describe a time when you wished for something and got it—and then wished you hadn't.

260. Major life events like a new job, a new home, the birth of a sibling, or the death of someone we love can have a profound impact on us. Describe a major event in your life and what it taught you about yourself or others.

261. People often say, "What you don't know won't hurt you," but the opposite often turns out to be true. Tell about a time when you were hurt by something you didn't know.

262. Parents are our first and most important teachers. Describe a time when you learned a valuable lesson from one of your parents.

263. Recall a time when you found yourself in a perilous situation. Tell the story of how you got into that situation and how you survived it.

264. We often discover something we didn't know about ourselves (or others) when we are forced to handle an unexpected situation. Describe a time when you were faced with something unexpected and what you learned in the process.

265. Many experiences in our lives are memorable because they forced us to examine our basic beliefs and values. Tell about such an experience in your life.

266. Many writers have dealt with the theme of a character losing control and going beyond reason. Describe a time in your life when you lost control, and tell why.

267. Preconceived notions often turn out to be false. Describe a time when you discovered that a preconceived notion of yours (about a person, place, or thing) was wrong.

268. It isn't always easy to do what is right, and sometimes it can even be dangerous. Describe a time when you put yourself at risk (physically, socially, emotionally, or professionally) to do what you thought was right.

269. Some of our richest experiences take place when we travel. Tell about a memorable experience you had when you were traveling.

270. Sometimes we take nature for granted. Describe an experience that made you appreciate the natural world.

271. The first time we try something new can be exciting, frightening, and enlightening. Tell about an important "first" in your life and what you learned from the experience.

272. Animals can sometimes seem remarkably human. Describe an experience with an animal that acted in a very human way.

273. Most of us have to make many difficult choices throughout our lives. Describe a time when you had to make a tough decision.

274. It has often been said that "Life is a journey, not a destination." Tell about an important journey (physical, emotional, or spiritual) that you've taken.

275. How people handle a problem often reveals a lot about their character. Describe a time you encountered a difficult problem and how you solved it.

276. **It has been said that the truth is often stranger than fiction. Describe an experience you had that was so strange others might think you made it up.**

277. It is often said that you should never judge another person until you walk in his or her shoes. Tell about an experience that enabled you to better understand another person.

278. **We all have things that we are afraid of, and sometimes we find ourselves in situations that force us to face our deepest fears. Tell about a time when you had to face one of your greatest fears.**

279. Sometimes we surprise ourselves with what we are able to do. Describe a time when you accomplished something you didn't think you could do.

280. When we are faced with challenges and difficult situations, we sometimes discover strengths we did not know we had. Tell about a time when you recognized a new strength in yourself.

281. Sometimes change can be intimidating—especially technological change. Describe a time when you had difficulty with a new technology.

282. No matter how well we prepare, sometimes, unexpected things may happen. Other times, we may simply be unable to prepare. Tell about a time when you were unprepared for a situation.

283. Some of our most memorable moments are when we achieve an important goal. Tell about a time when you accomplished a goal you had been working toward.

284. Sometimes something negative turns out to be positive—a "blessing in disguise." Describe a time in your life when something bad turned out to be good.

285. **Moving can be a very exciting but also difficult time in one's life. Tell about a time you moved and how it affected you.**

286. When we are unhappy with a situation, we can either accept it or do something to change it. Tell about a time when you initiated change.

287. We often learn a great deal from our failures. Describe a time when you failed and what you learned from the experience.

288. **As the saying goes, "If at first you don't succeed, try, try again." Describe a time when you persisted until you achieved your goal.**

289. Many people believe that it is better to have loved and lost than to never have loved at all. Tell about an experience that shows this statement to be true.

290. Most people believe that there are certain things worth fighting for. Tell about a time when you fought for something you believed in.

291. From the time we are toddlers, we begin to challenge authority to test our limits. Describe a time when you challenged authority.

292. **Movies and literature often deal with the theme of "counting your blessings." Tell about an experience that led you to appreciate someone or something you'd taken for granted.**

293. Even if we know money can't buy us happiness, we are often disappointed when we are unable to afford something we desire. Describe a time when you could not afford something you deeply desired.

294. Our first foray into the world of work is bound to generate some interesting experiences. Tell about a memorable incident from your first job.

295. We often put people we admire so high on a pedestal that we forget they're human. Describe a time when you realized that someone you admired was imperfect.

296. Though some say, "rules are meant to be broken," breaking the rules often has serious consequences. Tell about a time when you broke the rules and what happened as a result.

297. In many situations, as the saying goes, "two heads are better than one." Describe a time when you accomplished something through teamwork that you could not have achieved on your own.

298. People often say, "It's better to be safe than sorry." Tell about an experience that proves this saying to be true.

299. Sometimes the course of our lives can change in an instant. Describe an experience that changed the direction of your life.

300. Tell about a time when you found something important that you thought you had lost.

301. Once words are uttered, it's impossible to take them back. Describe a time when you said something you wish you had not.

302. First impressions are often very important. Describe a time you got (or gave) the wrong first impression.

303. In one of his most famous lines, Shakespeare's Hamlet says, "I must be cruel, only to be kind." Describe a time when you, too, had to be cruel to be kind.

304. **We are often surprised, even awed, by the experiences of our ancestors. Describe a time when you learned something important about your family history.**

305. Unfortunately, conflicts over money have the power to destroy even the strongest of relationships. Describe a time when you had a conflict over money.

306. There are many sides to every story. Tell about a time when many people were involved in a conflict.

307. Have you ever forgotten something very important? Tell about your experience.

308. When we meet someone we haven't seen in a long time, we are often surprised by how much they have changed. Describe a time when this happened to you.

309. Describe a time when you received a valuable gift.

310. **Most of us remember exactly where we were and what we were doing when we received shocking or important news. Tell the story of what you were doing when you heard about an important event and how that news affected you.**

311. Some people believe that you should seize the day—take every opportunity to live life to its fullest. Describe a time when you decided to seize the day.

312. The quality of our character is often reflected in how much we are willing to sacrifice for others. Describe a time when you sacrificed for someone else.

313. Tell about an experience you had while volunteering your help.

314. Sometimes the extraordinary can happen during the most ordinary of tasks. Describe your experience.

315. It is often both frightening and exciting to do something on our own for the first time. Tell about a time when you first did something on your own.

316. Holidays are meant to be special occasions, and they are often very emotional. Describe an event from a particularly memorable holiday.

317. For many of us, sports are a big part of our lives, whether we are spectators or participants. Describe a memorable sporting event.

318. It is often said that "The greatest risk is not taking one." Tell about a time when you took a chance.

319. For many of us, our roles—as parents or children, supervisors or subordinates, teachers or students—are very clearly defined. But sometimes the tables turn, and we end up switching roles with another. Tell about a time when you experienced a role reversal.

320. **Many things can interfere with our plans. Sometimes an illness prevents us from doing something we really want to do. Describe a time when you became ill and missed out on doing something you'd really been looking forward to.**

321. One of Robert Frost's most famous poems tells about a man who takes the road less traveled. Tell about a time when you also chose the less-traveled path.

322. We often learn valuable lessons in the workplace. Describe an experience at work that taught you something important.

323. It has been said that we can lie with silence as well as with words. Tell about a time when you "told" a lie by keeping silent about something important.

324. Sometimes a simple misunderstanding can lead to a major conflict. Describe a time when this happened to you.

325. **Many of our fondest memories are associated with food. Describe a memorable experience that took place while preparing or eating food.**

326. Some of our most memorable experiences take place outdoors, away from the comforts of home. Write about a memorable experience you had while in the great outdoors.

327. Many people believe that hatred is our most destructive emotion. Describe an experience that proves this statement to be true.

328. Louis D. Brandeis said, "Behind every argument is someone's ignorance." Describe a time when someone's lack of knowledge led to an argument.

329. Most of us have done things we didn't want to do because of pressure from our peers. Tell about a time that you gave in to peer pressure.

330. There is a bumper sticker that reads, "Perform random acts of kindness." Describe a time when you performed or witnessed a random act of kindness.

331. Tell about a time when you left the safety of a place or situation to explore or try something new.

332. Sometimes an experience can trigger a powerful memory of someone or something from your past. Describe a time when this happened to you.

333. Tell about an experience that prepared you to help someone in a challenging situation.

334. Baltasar Gracian, a Spanish philosopher, once said that, "The things we remember best are those best forgotten." Describe an experience you wish you'd never had.

335. The French playwright, Molière, wrote, "The greater the obstacle the more glory in overcoming it." Tell about a time you overcame a great difficulty.

336. Describe an experience that led you to change a long-held opinion.

337. As children, our strongest bonds are usually with our parents and then with our siblings. Tell about a memorable experience with one of your siblings or a close relative.

338. Superheroes, like Spiderman, don't use weapons to subdue their foes. Rather, they rely upon a few special tools and their own ingenuity. Describe a time when your quick thinking saved the day.

339. We often have memorable experiences when we are learning a new skill or task. Describe an experience you had while learning something new.

340. There is a saying that states, "You can never go home again." Describe a time when you returned to a place from your past and how you and the place had changed.

341. Try as we might to avoid them, accidents happen. Tell about a time when you were involved in an accident.

342. Describe an experience you had that would be considered a near miss or a brush with disaster.

343. We learn many lessons from many different sources throughout our lives. Tell about a time you learned something that you can't learn from any book.

344. Some of our most difficult experiences are when we find ourselves stuck in a moral dilemma. Describe a time when this happened to you.

345. We are tested in many ways throughout our lives. Tell about a time when you were tested.

346. Describe a time when you enjoyed something you thought you would not like.

347. Television shows often depict family conflicts. Describe a time when you had a conflict with a family member.

348. Describe a time when you witnessed something unbelievable.

349. Many stories and essays describe the writer's school days. Tell about a memorable experience from your formal education.

350. Ours is a highly competitive society. Describe a time when you were involved in a heated contest.

351. Throughout our lives we may be asked to do things we do not want to do. Tell about a time when this happened to you.

352. As we grow older, we take on more and more responsibility. Describe a time when you were given a responsibility that you were not ready for.

353. In Robert Frost's poem "Mending Wall," a man tells his neighbor, "Good fences make good neighbors," suggesting that we need clear boundaries to get along. Describe an experience that proves this statement to be true.

354. It has often been said that there is nothing to fear but fear itself. Describe a time when you overcame one of your fears.

355. Sometimes when we meet someone, we have no idea how important that person will become to us later in our lives. Describe the time you first met someone who later became very important to you.

356. People sometimes say, "Either you're with us, or you're against us." Tell about a time when you had to choose between two sides.

357. It isn't always easy to be ourselves, especially when we are worried about what others may think of us. Tell about a time you pretended to be someone or something you were not.

358. Oscar Levant, a pianist and movie actor, said, "Happiness is not something you experience, it's something you remember." Describe an event that you are happy to remember.

359. We all need help from others from time to time. Tell about a time you helped someone in need.

360. Describe an experience that shows the accuracy of the following quotation: "Your luck is how you treat people."

361. Write about a time when you found something of significant emotional or monetary value.

362. Every culture has its own rites of passage. Describe your experience with a rite of passage in your culture.

363. As much as we may love our friends, we sometimes find ourselves very angry with them. Tell about a time when you had a conflict with a close friend.

364. Some people prefer to play it safe; others are always ready to take chances. Describe a time when you decided to take a chance.

365. If you have ever been treated unfairly, you may have been told, "Who ever said life has to be fair?" Describe a time you were treated unfairly and how you handled the situation.

366. Have you ever befriended someone simply because he or she looked like he needed a friend? Describe your experience.

367. When parents set limits and discipline their children, they often say, "Someday, you'll understand why I'm doing this." Tell about a time when you realized that your parents were doing what they thought was best, even though it made you very angry at the time.

368. If you could be invisible for one day, what would you do? Write a story detailing the events of this imaginary day.

369. P.W. Litchfield, founder of Goodyear Tire & Rubber, wrote, "One realizes the full importance of time only when there is little of it left." Describe an experience in your life that proved this statement to be true.

370. Many stories, like Stephen Crane's "The Open Boat," talk about the indifference of nature to human needs and desires. Talk about a time in your life when you experienced nature's indifference to your needs.

371. Alexander Maclaren, a Baptist minister, said, "The man who has not learned to say *no* will be a weak, if not a wretched man, as long as he lives." Describe an experience when you should have said *no*, but did not.

372. Our dreams often reflect our subconscious fears and desires. Tell about a time you had a very troubling or enlightening dream.

373. Certain key experiences help us mature from children into young adults. Describe one of those key experiences in your life.

374. Few things give us as much pleasure as creating something beautiful. Tell about a time when you created something.

375. Many conversations begin with the introduction, "You'll never guess who I bumped into today . . ." Chance meetings can make for very interesting experiences. Describe a time when you bumped into someone, and it led to a memorable conversation or event.

376. Music can often trigger powerful memories. Describe a memorable experience associated with a particular song or piece of music.

RUBRIC FOR NARRATIVE WRITING

Score	6	5	4	3	2	1
	For a grade at this level, your writing:	For a grade at this level, your writing:	For a grade at this level, your writing:	For a grade at this level, your writing:	For a grade at this level, your writing:	For a grade at this level, your writing:
Content: Your written response shows an understanding and interpretation of the writing prompt.	▪ satisfies the requirements of the writing prompt in a creative and original manner. ▪ uses an obvious theme throughout.	▪ provides a thoughtful analysis of the writing prompt. ▪ uses a clear theme throughout.	▪ meets some of the requirements of the writing prompt. ▪ includes some key elements that help explain the thesis.	▪ offers a simple interpretation of the writing prompt. ▪ lacks a theme.	▪ meets few of the requirements of the writing prompt. ▪ discusses very basic ideas. ▪ makes few connections to help explain the thesis.	▪ minimally addresses the writing prompt. ▪ digresses, repeats, or dwells on insignificant details throughout.
Development: Your written response gives a clear and logical explanation of ideas, using supporting material.	▪ builds and elaborates ideas thoroughly. ▪ uses examples precisely. ▪ develops the topic in an interesting and imaginative way. ▪ demonstrates coherence in the development of ideas.	▪ develops the topic in an acceptable way. ▪ uses relevant examples throughout the essay. ▪ develops ideas clearly and consistently.	▪ answers the question in an abbreviated manner. ▪ gives brief examples to explain ideas.	▪ shows weakness in the development of ideas and/or develops ideas without thorough explanation.	▪ contains inaccurate, vague, or repetitive details. ▪ has limited development of ideas.	▪ shows a lack of development of ideas.
Organization: Your written response shows a coherent, orderly, well-reasoned approach.	▪ sets up and maintains a clear focus. ▪ establishes a logical, rational sequence of ideas with transitional words and sentences.	▪ has an obvious plan of organization. ▪ focuses on the thesis statement. ▪ uses appropriate devices and transitions.	▪ has a general focus. ▪ has an obvious attempt at organization. ▪ exhibits a logical sequence of ideas.	▪ does not show a logical sense of organization. ▪ strays from the topic. ▪ can be difficult to follow.	▪ shows an attempt to create a focus. ▪ digresses from the topic. ▪ is disorganized.	▪ is less organized than a 2-point response. ▪ exhibits no organizational pattern or focus.
Conventions/ Language Use: Your written response shows a sense of audience by using effective vocabulary and varied sentence structure.	▪ has vivid language, fluidity, and a sense of engagement and voice. ▪ has sophisticated style of sentence structure, sentence variety, and vocabulary. ▪ has essentially no errors.	▪ has good control of mechanics. ▪ contains some errors when using sophisticated language ▪ has a slightly lower quality of sentence structure and sentence variety. ▪ shows errors when using sophisticated vocabulary only.	▪ has a sense of audience. ▪ uses simple sentences. ▪ uses an appropriate level of vocabulary. ▪ demonstrates partial control of mechanics. ▪ exhibits some errors that do not interfere with comprehension.	▪ uses vocabulary that is slightly below level. ▪ has a vague sense of audience. ▪ shows a beginner's control of the language. ▪ has errors that begin to interfere with comprehension.	▪ exhibits little control of the language. ▪ has errors that make comprehension difficult.	▪ shows minimal control of language skills. ▪ may be illegible or unrecognizable as English.

A ZERO PAPER is:

▪ totally unrelated to the topic.

▪ filled with indecipherable words and is illegible.

▪ incoherent with illogical or garbled syntax.

▪ blank.

Scoring Explanations for Narrative Writing Essays

A score of "**6**" indicates that your essay satisfies the requirements of the writing prompt in a creative and original manner, using an obvious theme throughout. You thoroughly articulate your ideas in a coherent fashion, use precise examples, and develop the topic in an interesting manner. The narrative uses dialogue effectively, contains believable characters, and conveys vivid emotions and situations. The story itself is orderly with a clear focus, a logical sequence of ideas, and transitional words and sentences. Your writing demonstrates a sense of audience by using effective vocabulary, varied sentence structure, and fluid, sophisticated language that is essentially without errors.

A score of "**4**" indicates that your essay meets some of the requirements of the writing prompt but develops ideas somewhat inconsistently. Your essay may answer the question in an abbreviated manner, using little dialogue, and giving only brief examples to support the thesis. Your essay has a general focus, makes an obvious attempt at organization, and presents your ideas in a logical sequence. The language of your essay indicates a general control of mechanics but has a slightly lower quality of sentence structure and variety. An essay of this type contains errors only when using sophisticated language.

A score of "**1**" indicates that the essay only minimally addresses the writing prompt, digressing, repeating, or dwelling on insignificant details throughout. Your essay shows a lack of development and exhibits no organizational pattern or focus. Your language skills may be illegible or unrecognizable as English.

Model Narrative Writing Essays

254. People often say "Don't judge a book by its cover." Describe a time when you misjudged someone based on his or her appearance or when someone misjudged you.

Sample 6 Score

When Maria Mariella Panontin first showed up at our school, here's what I thought: *Look at that girl. She dresses like she's some exotic gypsy or something. Looks like a real high-maintenance kind of girl. Not my type; I'm not going to bother trying to get to know her.*" So I didn't. Too late, I realized what a mistake I'd made.

Maria Mariella (she went by both names) was a foreign exchange student from Italy who was staying with a friend of mine, Joanne. Joanne and I weren't that close, but we hung out in the same general crowd, so when the extended clique got together, Maria Mariella was often part of the group. We were friendly to each other, but we never tried to become friends until Shanda's party.

I wasn't planning on going to Shanda's party because I had a big track meet the next day, but my friend Elaine convinced me to go for a little while. When I was saying goodbye, Joanne rushed up to me.

"Hey, Jenine, can you do me a really big favor? Maria Mariella needs to go home, but I want to stay. Would you mind dropping her off at my house?"

I didn't really want to, but it was on the way, and I would have looked like a real jerk if I said no, so I said, "Sure, no problem." Maria Mariella was right behind Joanne. I looked at her and said, "Let's go."

We hopped into my car. As I was pulling out of the driveway, I popped in a 10,000 Maniacs cassette and turned the radio up loud.

"I love this song!" Maria Mariella shouted over the music.

"Really?" Not even my American friends appreciated this band. "You like the 10,000 Maniacs?"

"I love them," she said with her heavy Italian accent.

After that, it seemed like Maria Mariella and I couldn't stop talking to one another and finding things in common. I loved that she was straightforward and honest, like me. She shared my taste in music and film. We both had crushes on the same movie stars. It felt like a friendship that was meant to be.

Then, just two weeks later, Maria Mariella threw a party at Joanne's house. It was a going away party. Her mother had developed a serious illness, and Maria Mariella was going home to be with her. At that party, a group of us were playing Truth or Dare, one of our favorite games. It was Maria Mariella's turn.

"Truth!" she said.

"Name something you regret," our friend Denise demanded.

Maria Mariella pointed a long finger at me. "I wish I'd taken the time to get to know you sooner. I didn't think you were worth my time."

A sad smile came across my face. "I thought the same thing, Maria Mariella," I said. "That is something I'm always going to regret."

Sample 4 Score

They say you shouldn't judge a book by it's cover, but people often do. I learned my lesson about this in high school when I met Maria Mariella. I didn't think she was worth getting to know but I was very wrong. She turned out to be a great friend, but by the time I realized it she was gone.

Maria Mariella came to our school from Italy, she stayed with a friend of mine, Joanne. I saw Maria Mariella a lot at school and parties but I never really talked to her. Just from how she looked and dressed (like a gypsy), I didn't think I'd like her. Then one night Joanne asked me to take Maria Mariella home because I was leaving early and she wanted to leave early too. So I did, and I found out she loved the 10,000 Maniacs as much as I did, not even my best friend liked the same music. After that we started talking and hanging out, and we kept finding that we had all kinds of things in common. The more we talked, the more we liked each other.

Its a sad thing that our friendship was so short. Maria Mariella had to go back to Italy a few weeks later because her mother got sick. At her good-bye party, we were playing "Truth or Dare." It was our favorite game. When it was Maria Mariella's turn she said "truth." Denise asked her to tell the truth about something she regrets.

Maria Mariella said, "I wish I'd gotten to know you sooner, I didn't think you were worth my time." I said, me too, and that's something we both regret.

Sample 1 Score

One time I misjudeged someone based on their appearance and someone misjudged me also. In high school. We shouldn't not to judge other people because it is wrong, you must to get to know some body first and then you can have an opinion on them what there like. When you judge some one first you can be a lot wrong in fact really wrong about what that person is to be like. For example, Maria Mariella, in high school. I didn't not liked her because I thought she looked stupid the way she dressing up all the time. Although she really was nice. It was too late.

Don't not judge a book by its cover, it can make you very sad.

276. It has been said that the truth is often stranger than fiction. Describe an experience you had that was so strange others might think you made it up.

*Note: The name of the celebrity in this narrative has to remain anonymous because it is a true story.

Sample 6 Score

My friends still think I made this story up, even though they've never known me to be a liar. When it happened I couldn't believe it myself, but it's true. This really happened.

My best friend and I were working one summer as line chefs in the Marriott at the sprawling TanTara Resort on the Lake of the Ozarks, Missouri. One Tuesday morning, as I walked through the kitchen to get to the time clock, half a dozen people said to me, "Uh-oh, man, the executive chef wants to see you." The executive chef? But I hadn't done anything wrong. What could he want? Why was I in trouble?

I clocked in and knocked on the executive chef's door. "Listen," he said angrily when I sat down, "I don't know what you guys did or how you did it, but you and your buddy Jim have off on Friday." Friday was our busiest night; no one gets off on Friday without a *very* good reason. "Just one thing," he said sternly as I got up to go, "Don't you guys tell anyone why you're not coming in. Understand?"

"Understand," I replied, but I had no idea what he was talking about. I had to find Jim as soon as possible and figure out what was going on. But every time I asked Jim about it, he simply said, "I'll tell you later. Just don't worry about it." No matter how much I begged, he wouldn't tell me what was going on and why we had the day off. By Thursday night, he still hadn't told me what was happening Friday. As we were watching TV in our apartment, he said, "Let's hit the sack early tonight. We're going to need lots of rest for tomorrow." Jim never went to bed early. What on earth was going on?

In the morning, Jim woke me up (another anomaly) and told me to get a quick shower, put on my bathing suit, and pack a change of clothes. A few minutes later, a dark SUV with tinted windows pulled up in front of our building. "There's our ride," Jim said with a secretive smile. We walked out to the car, but I wasn't getting in without an explanation. So Jim shoved me in. Inside, I looked up, and there in the passenger seat was _____.

Now Jim had no choice but to explain. It turns out that a friend of a friend of Jim's knew _____ and knew that _____ wanted to get away for a totally private vacation between films. This friend said that he knew two guys at a large secluded lake in Missouri who would "take care of him." So ____ called the executive chef and asked for me and Jim to have the day off.

We spent the day out on the lake with _____, water-skiing, fishing, eating, drinking, and telling stories. We did our best to treat him like just another guy spending the day with a couple of new friends. We didn't ask him anything about Hollywood or his latest high-profile romance; we just let him relax and be himself for a day without cameras or fans.

At the end of the day, as we pulled back into the dock, he said, "Listen, guys, I had a really good time today. It was just what I needed. I appreciate it, man." He shook our hands. "One favor, though?" he asked. "Don't tell anybody about this. If people find out I'm here, I won't get any peace and quiet. I need some time alone."

"No problem," we said, and headed home. The next day, everyone kept asking what was so special that we had to have Friday off. The night was a disaster for the kitchen, and they were all upset that we hadn't been there. All we could say was, "Nothing, man, nothing. We were just hanging out." We had a great time, too, and we kept our promise.

Sample 4 Score

My friends still don't believe me when I tell them this story, but its true. I was working in a restaurant at a big lake resort, in Missouri, when my boss called me into his office. I thought I was in trouble. Instead, he told me that me and my roommate and best friend, Jim, had Friday off. Normally you have to beg and plead or have an emergency to have a Friday off, here I was getting the day off without even asking. I had no idea what was going on. He seems angry, too, and says, "don't you and your friend tell anybody why your not coming in Friday, understand"? I said yes, but I was clueless.

I kept asking my roommate about it but he decides not to tell me anything. "Just don't worry," he keeps saying, and it was starting to drive me crazy. For three days, he kept the secret. Then, Friday morning, he wakes me up early (I'm always the one up first, so I thought this was really weird) and tells me to get dressed. A few minutes later, a black SUV with dark windows pulls up, and he tells me to get in. No way, I say, but he pushes me in, and that's when I see whose in the car, _____.

"What is going on?" I demand so I finally get my explanation. A friend of a friend of Jim heard that _____ needed a vacation between movies, told him to go to this lake which is pretty private because its really big, you can hide away there if you want. He also gave _____ our names and said we would take care of him for the day if he wanted, so he called our boss and told him to give us the day off. We went out on the lake then and spent the day out on the boat.

It turns out that _____ was a really cool guy. It was hard to treat him like just another guy, but we did, because that was what he wanted. We didn't ask him about his movies or anything, actually he kept asking us questions about us. We all had a great time. At the end of the day, he thanks us and asks us not to tell anyone so that people don't chase him with cameras and stuff. We promised. It was so hard not to tell anyone what we did that day!

Sample 1 Score

Some people they make up storys all the time, you don't know when to beleive them if its true or not. Some time, the storys are super strange like it couldn't really of happened in the first place, then no body is going to beleive it. One time a story like that happen to me, when I met an actor, he was on vacation and asks my boss for me to have the day off. So me and my friend could hang out with him. But we're not aloud to tell any body any thing. That was so frustrating! For me.

This guy he was a really good actor, I seen him in a lot of films, I was like wow when I met him but I have to play it cool, like I don't care how famous he is. That was so hard. We hung out all day and he was a really nice guy to. He was glad noone else knows that he is there on the lake or else they all come after him with cameras and stuff and bother him a lot.

278.   We all have things that we are afraid of, and sometimes we find ourselves in situations that force us to face our deepest fears. Tell about a time when you had to face one of your greatest fears.

Sample 6 Score

Every kid in the neighborhood knew the Robinson house and avoided it like a bowl of Brussels sprouts. Mr. Robinson was a notorious crank, the house was always dark and creepy, and his dog was a terror—a mean, fang-toothed creature that looked like she would love to tear you apart.

The dog's name was Angel, but she scared the devil out of us. She was half pit bull, half Doberman pinscher. Mr. Robinson kept her out on the front lawn, chained to a thin pole stuck in the ground near his front door. It was a long chain, and when I walked past the house to the bus stop, Angel always bounded toward me, barking furiously. *One of these times that chain will break*, I thought, *and I'll be Angel's dinner*. When I got to the Robinson house, I always walked past it as quickly as I could. Sometimes I could see Mr. Robinson watching from the window, laughing.

Then it happened. We had gotten our report cards in school that day, and I was so proud of my marks and my teachers' comments that I just had to look at them again on my way home from the bus stop. I was so wrapped up in that report card that I didn't realize how close I was to Mr. Robinson's house, and Angel startled me when she started barking. I dropped my report card, and just then, a big gust of wind took the paper up into the air. It landed right smack in the middle of Mr. Robinson's lawn, about two feet away from Angel.

Angel, growling ferociously, was straining her chain, trying to get closer to me. I could see her long canines. I could even smell her from where I was standing. I think I was shaking. But I needed to get that report card back. My mom had to sign it. Besides, she had to see those fantastic grades.

I thought about yelling for Mr. Robinson, but I was just as afraid of him as of the dog. So I decided to see if maybe, just maybe, Angel would let me get close enough to get that piece of paper.

I remembered my uncle telling me that dogs can sense your fear, and that most dogs will be friendly if you approach them in the right manner. So I did my best not to look scared. I straightened up, softened my face, and walked slowly toward Angel. She kept barking and growling. Saliva was dripping from her chin. I closed my eyes and gulped. I was about six feet away from Angel, and I put my fist out in front of me for her to smell, saying, "Here, girl. Nice girl. Good girl," as calmly as I could. But she was barking so loudly and angrily that I'm sure she didn't hear a word.

Inside, I had never been more frightened. *This dog is going to tear me to pieces*, I thought. But I kept going, slowly. I had never earned such good marks before. I wasn't going to let a crazy old dog keep me from showing that report card to my parents.

I was about three steps away from Angel when the wind blew again, this time sending my report card just out of Angel's reach. I didn't have to confront that dog after all. It was a good thing, too—Mr. Robinson later told my folks that Angel surely would have bitten me badly. I realized that what I'd planned to do was dangerous and that I was simply being stubborn. But part of me was proud, because I was brave enough to try to get close to Angel.

Sample 4 Score

Growing up, a dog named Angel was one of my biggest fears. She was a vicious dog, half pit bull and half Doberman pincher. I had to walk past her house a lot, and every time I did, I walked as fast as I could. Sometimes I saw her owner, Mr. Robinson, watching out the window. He was as creepy as she was mean.

One day we got our report cards and I saw I'd gotten the best grades ever. I couldn't wait to show my parents. On my way home, passing the Robinsons house, I was looking at my report card again. I was just so proud. But then Angel started to bark, and that scared me. I dropped my report card, and some wind came along and blew it right next to Angel.

Angel was pulling on her chain and growling at me, scaring me to death. But, I had to get my report card back. What was I going to do? I decided to try to make friends with Angel. I know that if you hold your hand out to a dog and don't act scared they'll often be friendly to you because then they don't fell threatened. So, I slowly approached Angel trying not to look to scared. I thought she was going to attack me, but I kept going slowly towards her.

Luckily, just then the wind blew again. This time my report card blew towards me and far enough away from Angel that I could get it safely. I breathed a big sigh of relief and headed home. Later Mr. Robinson told my parents that Angel surely would have bitten me. It's a good thing I didn't get any closer. Still I'm proud that I got as close as I did.

Sample 1 Score

Dogs can be really scarey. In my neighborhood they're was a really scarey dog named "Angel." She was mean and always barking. Everyone was scared of her. We all thought her owner Mr. robinson was weird too and scarey. He was always peaking out of his windows and watching.

One day when I was coming home from school. My report card blue out of my hands next to Angel. I was really scared, more then ever. I got close and then the wind blue again, luckily for me. She just kept barking and growling all the time, too. I was sure her chain would brake.

285. Moving can be a very exciting but also difficult time in one's life. Tell about a time you moved and how it affected you.

Sample 6 Score

As the new kid in town, I was eager—ok, desperate—to make new friends, and fast. My dad had just accepted a promotion that required a transfer, and we moved from Chicago to Oakland, California, just a few days before I was to begin the sixth grade. I didn't even have a chance to get to know any of the kids in the neighborhood.

After the first day of school, I could tell that Charlie Jenkins was the one who would make me or break me. He was a bully for sure, but he was so good-looking and charming that everyone seemed to like him. He was clearly the center of power in that classroom, and I knew I would have to win his approval. I just wasn't sure what I'd have to do to get it.

My answer came at the end of the third week of school, when Ms. Harcourt gave us our second writing assignment. We'd been reading and discussing fables, and now it was our turn to write our own. That afternoon, Charlie cornered me on the playground.

He teased me about being a new kid, yet he seemed interested in the fact that I was a good writer. Our teacher, Ms. Harcourt had read aloud one of my poems in class just yesterday, and obviously he was paying attention. I admitted that I had a flair for writing, and at first I was flattered that he noticed. But, he had an ulterior motive.

"Hey, new kid, hold on a second," he said, standing between the gate and me. "You seem to be pretty good with writing."

"Yeah, you do alright, alright," he replied. "I'll tell you what," he said, moving closer, until his face was just a few inches from mine. "Why don't you just write an extra fable, one for you, one for me? Let me see what you can do."

So that was it. I was going to do Charlie's English homework for him. That was the price I was going to pay to be accepted.

Charlie didn't wait for an answer. "Bring two fables to school on Monday," he said. That would give him time to copy it over into his own handwriting to submit to Ms. Harcourt on Tuesday.

Over the weekend, I wrote two fables, both of them quite good, I thought, but one was definitely better than the other. On Monday morning, I met Charlie in the schoolyard as planned.

"Here's your fable," I said to Charlie, handing him a piece of paper. I gave Charlie the fable that I thought was inferior, keeping the better fable for myself, and turned to walk away.

He questioned me about the quality of the paper, read it quickly, and decided that it passed muster. Without saying thank you or goodbye, he swaggered off into the building.

A few days later, Ms. Harcourt returned our fables. I looked at my paper, expecting to see an A or A+, but my grade was an A-. Then I looked over at Charlie. He was holding his paper up high so I could see his grade: A+. I knew the fable I'd kept for myself was better. Perhaps Charlie's charm was factored into his grade.

Fortunately, I only had to do one more assignment for Charlie before he and his family abruptly moved to another town. Now Charlie was going to be the new kid in the classroom. I often wondered what he had to do there to be accepted.

Sample 4 Score

One of the hardest things about moving is trying to make new friends. When we moved to Oakland, I didn't have time to make any friends before school started. I was the "new" kid in the classroom. The most popular kid in the sixth grade was Charlie, and I had to make sure he liked me. I could tell right away you wouldn't want Charlie as your enemy.

After a couple weeks of school, we were given an assignment in English, we had to write our own fables. (We'd been studying fables in class). Charlie came up to me in the playground that day. He'd found out I was a good writer, and he said I better write an extra fable for him. If I wanted Charlie to like me, I was going to have to do his English homework for him. "Meet me here Monday before school starts, with my fable," he said.

So I wrote two fables that weekend. Both of them were good, but one was better than the other. That's the one I kept for myself. I gave the other one to Charlie, outside of school on Monday morning, just like he said. He made me stand there while he read it to make sure it was good. He seemed to like it, and he let me go.

A few days later we get our fables back, and I couldn't believe it. Charlie got an A+ on his fable while I got an A-. I know my fable was better than his (which was really mine, of course). Maybe the teacher really liked Charlie. That's the only way I can explain it.

A few weeks later Charlie's family had to move, so I only had to do one more assignment for him. Now he had to be the new kid. I wonder how he handled it.

Sample 1 Score

Moving is a hard thing. It is often very difficult for family's. Especially children. I remember a time we moved. It affect me strongly. I had to do someone elses schoolwork. He ask me to do his assinment and I have to or else he wont like me and he is the most popular.

I do his homework for him and mine too. Then even though mine is better he gets an even better grade! This was not fare at all. I think the teacher had a big problem. Sometimes the popular kids are even poplar with teechers, they get better grades for nothing. This made me very angry.

I was very happy when he moved away then I didn't have to do any more work for him or worry if he likes me.

288. As the saying goes, "If at first you don't succeed, try, try again." Describe a time when you persisted until you achieved your goal.

Sample 6 Score

In seventh grade, I had a best friend who was an incredible athlete. I was pretty coordinated myself, but because I was so insecure, I never seemed to be any good at sports. I was so afraid of missing the ball that I would be sure to swing and miss, even if it was right over the plate. But Katie was my best friend, and if she joined a team, I did, too. Or at least I tried. Katie was a starter for the junior varsity field hockey team; I sat on the bench all season. Katie played regularly in JV basketball; I was cut during tryouts. I figured I was headed for a similar fate with lacrosse. But Katie was my best friend, so I signed up anyway.

Katie was a natural, and she picked up the new sport quickly. I, on the other hand, couldn't seem to hold the lacrosse stick comfortably. I caught one out of ten throws, if I was lucky, and my tosses were always way off their mark. I was clumsy and feeling clumsier, and I thought maybe it was time to give it up. But that would create an even wider gulf between Katie and me. Already she was spending more and more time with the girls who, like her, excelled at sports. I was beginning to be left behind.

Determined to stick it out and save our friendship, I begged my mom to take me to a sporting goods store and buy me an early birthday present: my own lacrosse stick and ball so I could practice at home. Katie was impressed with my stick, but I could tell that she thought it was a waste of money. She figured I would never get to use that stick in a game.

I was hurt by her reaction, and again I felt the distance between us. If I was going to keep Katie as a friend, I thought, I simply *had* to get the hang of this sport. It was my last chance. Somehow, someway, I had to learn how to throw and catch the ball in that net and be respectable on the playing field.

So I practiced, and I practiced, and I practiced some more. I often felt like there was no hope, and I broke two windows in the garage, but I kept at it.

Then, one day, just after the first official game of the season (during which I sat on the bench), something happened. I paired off with Suzie, who had become my partner since Katie had quickly proven to be too good to play with me. That day, when Suzi sent me her first throw, I caught it. When I threw the ball back to her, I hit her stick dead on. I caught her next throw, and the next. Something was happening. I was *getting* it. The stick was actually feeling good in my hands. The movements were becoming natural. I was catching and throwing the ball accurately.

I still don't know what exactly happened that day, but I will always be grateful for it. By the end of the season, I was starting for the JV team. I scored 12 goals that year, and the next year I was playing varsity. My success on the field gave me confidence that I desperately needed. Katie and I continued to drift apart, but Suzie turned out to be a great friend. She quit after the first year, but she came to every game to cheer me on.

Sample 4 Score

They say that if you don't succeed, try, try again until you do. When I was in Junior High School, I tried many sports because my best friend did. She was a great athlete; I was not. I sat on the bench all of field hockey season and I got cut during basketball tryouts, too. I stuck with it, though and finally made it on the lacrosse team.

My friend Katie picked up lacrosse right away, but I struggled. Even though she was my best friend I couldn't be partners with her during practice. Because she was so much better than me. I was afraid that if I didn't learn how to be good at lacrosse, our friendship would be over. She was spending more and more time with her sports friends, and I was feeling more and more left out.

I decided to do something to save our friendship. I went out and bought a lacrosse stick. After practice, I'd come home and practice. I practiced on weekends, too. I tried and tried and tried. Some days I felt like there wasn't any hope, but I kept trying.

Then one day, it happened. I was throwing and catching the ball with Suzie, my new partner. Suddenly, I caught the ball. I caught the next one she threw, too. My throws to her were accurate. From that day on, I got better and better. I had more confidence, too. I ended up playing a lot that season on the JV team and even scored 12 goals. Suzie quit the team, but she was my new friend, and she came to cheer me on. I'm really glad I kept trying.

Sample 1 Score

As the saying goes if at first you don't succeed try try again. This is good advise to everyone. I try and try and try until I get good at lacross.

This is a fun sport, I really enjoy it. You have to throw and catch the ball in a net. When I first start I was lousy at it. I couldnt catch or through the ball right. I was sitting on the bench all the time. My friend was really good at it. She even plays varsity her first year.

This friend shes looking for other friends who are like her good at sports not like me. She really hurt me a lot that way. However I make new friends like Suzie. She was my partner in practices. She stayed with me even when I learned how to play right.

292. Movies and literature often deal with the theme of "counting your blessings." Tell about an experience that led you to appreciate someone or something you'd taken for granted.

Sample 6 Score

I often complained about our lack of wealth to my parents, who often replied that I had no idea what it means to be poor and that someday they'd show me what poverty was really like. I thought they were all talk, but one day, they proved me wrong—and showed me just how right they were, and they said I would see.

I did see, and the images from that day still haunt me. My parents were very active in their church, and they had arranged to deliver clothing and food donations to a church in a deeply impoverished area on the edge of the Appalachian Mountains, a four-hour drive from our home.

I'd seen pictures of poverty before, of course. But seeing a picture of a shack with seven malnourished children and actually walking into such a shack are two entirely different things. The pastor of the church took us into a few homes so we could deliver some of the items (a crib, a box of linens, canned goods) personally. I had never felt so uncomfortable before. These people had so little! Eight family members living in two rooms . . . no electricity or running water . . . no couches or microwaves or cable television . . . soon I began to realize just how lucky I was. True, I didn't have as much as my friends. But I had so much more than the people we visited that day. I felt greedy and guilty for having so many things.

When we got back home, I got on the Internet and found a soup kitchen not too far from our home. I've been volunteering there twice a week ever since. Two of my friends have joined me. Every time we go, we count our blessings.

Sample 4 Score

On one afternoon I'll never forget, my parents taught me to appreciate what I have. We lived in a very rich neighborhood but we ourselves were not rich, we were only middle class. Therefore I always felt like I was poor; compared to all my friends and their fancy houses and pools and cars. None of my friends had to work; but I had to work, to afford my car.

I guess my parents got tired, of me complaining, so one day they woke me up really early and took me on a long drive to a really poor neighborhood. I mean this place was really, really poor. I never saw such poverty before. The people, they lived in shacks, not houses. Everything was dirty, they had nothing like we have in our houses, most of them didn't even have running water or even electricity. And so many people living in such a little shack, with everyone on top of each other.

We went there to deliver some food and clothing donations to a church. The paster, he took us to some houses to deliver some of the food and clothes ourselves. Thus, I could see for myself how much I really had.

When I got back home, I found a soup kitchen I could go to help other people who really don't have anything, not even food to eat. They always remind me to count my blessings.

Sample 1 Score

I am told "to count your blessings" and appreciate someone or something that you'd taken for granted. Many movies and books are about this. I am sure you have seen some and read some. Like scary movies where people get killed can make us apreciate the blessing, we are still alive. Or a war movie, that were not fighting a war. When I went to a poor town once when I was in school I saw people even more poor than me. That made me sad, they live with so little. Compared to how much I have. All the time I felt poor since my friends, they were so rich.

304. We are often surprised, even awed, by the experiences of our ancestors. Describe a time when you learned something important about your family history.

Sample 6 Score

My dad wasn't the type to talk much about anything, and he was especially quiet about his past. There were a few things I knew: He'd come over from Hungary in 1956, after the Revolution. He'd fought with the rebels in Budapest. He was a toolmaker in Hungary, and he was a toolmaker here. He left behind his parents and 11 brothers and sisters, who still lived in the countryside. They exchanged letters once or twice a year. That was about all I knew.

The summer that I was fourteen, my dad received one of those letters. In it was the news that one of his brothers had died. Maybe it was the realization that he was so out of touch with his family. Maybe it was his own mortality he was facing. In any case, a few days after the letter came, he told me about his role in the Hungarian Revolution and his escape from Hungary.

The Hungarian Revolution began with a massive student protest on October 23, 1956, and ended just a few weeks later in November after the city was invaded by Soviet tanks and the rebellion crushed. My dad, just 22 years old, had decided to join the students who were protesting the Communist regime, and soon he was not just a protester but a soldier, and not just a soldier but an officer in the rebel army. "Wait a minute," he said, and he returned with a tattered copy of LIFE magazine's special issue devoted to the Hungarian Revolution. He flipped through the pages, showing me image after image of buildings demolished by bombs, rebels fighting on foot against tanks, bodies lying in the street. Then he found the picture he was looking for. "There," he said, pointing to a window in an abandoned, bullet-ridden building. "I was hiding in there, throwing Malotov cocktails at the Russian tanks."

It's a long and fascinating story, and I wanted to know all the details. How did he get involved? How did he escape? How close was he to being captured or killed? I had so many questions. But the question I wanted answered most was this: *Why* did he fight? At that age, I was just starting to find my footing in the swampy ground of ethics and moral stances. I was having a tough time figuring out what I believed in, and I wanted desperately to understand how someone could believe in something so strongly that he would be willing to die for it.

Why did he do it? There were a lot of reasons, he said. For one thing, the Communist regime was ruining the economy. As a toolmaker with several years of experience, he had a better salary than most, but still, he said, "I couldn't afford both clothes and food." If he respected the government, he would have been able to live with that. "But what I couldn't live with," he said, "was not being able to say what I wanted. The Communists, they had all kinds of restrictions on everything. You couldn't go to the next town without the proper permissions and papers. And you couldn't say anything, not *anything*, against the government, or else they'd put you in jail, or worse. They'd come and get you late at night and no one in your family would ever see you again." That's what happened to his best friend, Attila. He disappeared the night of September 22, and no one ever heard from him again.

My dad often complains about America. The politicians are crooks, criminals have too many rights, schools and parents aren't strict enough with children, and the taxes are "an abomination." But I don't need to remind him that at least in this country, he can complain as loudly as he pleases.

Sample 4 Score

The summer I was fourteen, I learned something about my dad. He never talked much and I didn't really know that much about him. After he found out about his brother dying back in Hungary, he must've felt like it was important for me to know more. He decided it was time to tell me about the Hungarian Revolution.

My dad was a toolmaker in Hungary. Because he didn't like the Communist government, he decided to join the protests led by students angry at the government. That's how the rebellion started. The communists wouldn't let anyone talk bad about the government, and the protesters were attacked. That started the fighting. He showed me pictures of the revolution with lots of destroyed buildings and people lying in the street. It was horrible. Because he was a little older than most of the students, my dad became an officer in the rebel army.

I wanted to know why he decided to fight. He told me that because of the communist government, he couldn't make enough money to buy food and clothes. He couldn't travel to another town without the right papers. The most important thing, though, was freedom of speech. He couldn't say what he wanted. He said that anyone who criticized the government would get taken away in the middle of the night and no one would see them again. That happened to his best friend. For my dad, that was the last straw.

My dad escaped with the other refugees, and he's been living in America ever since 1956. He complains about America a lot, especially the politicians. But he knows that here, no one is going to come and take him away for that.

Sample 1 Score

I was surprised by my dad when he told me about the Hungarian revelution he fought. I knew before that he fought but I didn't no anything else about it. It was a short war and the communists one. He was even an officer in the army. He didn't like to talk much so thats part of why I was so surprised.

One question I had, was, why did he fight. He said he didn't like the government and they'd take you away just for saying that. I can't imagine such a thing. I'd want to fight to. That's not the way it is here in America. This is a really grate country and I'm glad to live here.

310. Most of us remember exactly where we were and what we were doing when we received shocking or important news. Tell the story of what you were doing when you heard about an important event and how that news affected you.

Sample 6 Score

Every May the carnival came to town. It was the standard small-town fair: a ferris wheel, a fun house, a giant slide, and dozens of booths where you could buy greasy food and try to win cheap stuffed animals for your date.

That's where I was, with my date—sort of. We weren't actually in the fairgrounds. We were in his car in the parking lot, stealing some time together. I was 16, but I wasn't allowed to date, and I had the sort of father who just might come to the fair to check up on me to make sure I wasn't hanging out with any boys.

Keith had borrowed his mom's Buick Skylark, as usual. REO Speedwagon's "I Can't Fight This Feeling" was playing on the radio when Keith rather abruptly ended a kiss, interrupting what I thought had been a perfectly nice romantic moment.

"I have something to tell you," he said. He wouldn't look me in the eye. My heart dropped to the floor. *He's going to break up with me*, I thought in horror.

But that's not what happened. In fact, I never could have guessed at what Keith was about to tell me.

He took a deep breath and looked straight ahead at the windshield. "Your mom was married to someone else before she married your dad," he said softly. "You have an older brother. He lives in North Carolina."

I know what you're thinking, because it's exactly what I was wondering, too: *How on Earth did Keith <u>know</u>* this? He guessed what I was thinking, and said:

"My mom told me." Then, before I could ask, he added: "Edie told her." Edie was his mother's hairdresser.

Finding out that I had an older brother was a shock enough. To find out from my boyfriend, who found out from his mother, who found out from her hairdresser—that was just too much. I was too overwhelmed to respond.

After a few minutes of silence during which Keith held my hand, what Keith told me about how he found out began to make sense. Edie was the daughter of my dad's best friend, Samuel. Though our families were no longer close, when I was young, we spent a lot of time together. Edie and her older sister used to babysit my sister and me. It wouldn't be so unlikely for her to pick up a family secret or two.

Keith's mom had told him what Edie told her because she believed it was proof that I wasn't good enough to be his girlfriend. He wanted me to know about my brother, of course, but he also wanted me to know that he was going to have to cool it for a while until his mom got over it.

The next day, I told my mom that I knew about my brother. At first, she looked shocked; then she looked relieved, as if a tremendous burden had been lifted. She was glad I knew, although she was sorry about the way in which I'd found out. She gave me my brother's phone number and told me I could call whenever I was ready.

Today, my brother and I talk regularly, and he is one of my closest friends. One of these days, I have to thank Edie for being such a gossip.

Sample 4 Score

When the fair came to our town I went like I always did. There were rides and games. You could also buy lots of food. I enjoyed the fair, but this time I wasn't going on any rides. I was sitting with my boyfriend in his car in the parking lot.

I wasn't suppose to have a boyfriend. That's why we were hiding in his car. We were listening to music and talking and kissing. Suddenly Keith stopped. He said he had something to tell me. I got really scared. Is he going to break up with me, I wondered?

That's what I thought was going to happen. But he surprised me even more.

"You have an older brother," Keith told me. I was shocked. He told me that my mother had been married before she met my dad. I never knew this, and I wondered how on earth Keith knew this if I didn't even know. I asked him, and he said, "My mom told me."

How on earth did his mom know, I demanded. It turns out her hairdresser, of all people told her. I was confused. But then I remember her hair dresser is Edie, who used to babysit us when we were little. Edie's dad and my dad were best friends a long time ago. Maybe that's how Edie found out. She must have heard them talking about it one time.

I was very upset that Keith knew something my parents hid from me. His mom told him because she wants him to break up with me. She was thinking our family is bad because of this. Plus he wanted me to know about my older brother. Well, the next morning I talked to my mom, and she gives me my brothers number. She says sorry for not telling me earlier, and now me and my brother we are very good friends. I am glad Edie liked to gossip.

Sample 1 Score

I am going to the fare like it always is coming to town and find out a secret about my brother from my boyfriend. We are in his car. Because I am not a loud to have boyfriends, so we hide there from my dad in case he is checking up on me. Then my boyfriend tells me his mom's hairdressing lady tells her about my brother and she tells him. I am all confuse, I say so he explain my brother is from my mom being married before she meets my dad. How, does he know. His mom tells him since her hairdressing lady tells her so he can break up with me.

I have to ask my mom right a way after this then she is gladly to know about it for me. Now I call my brother all thetime, we are good friends.

320. Many things can interfere with our plans. Sometimes an illness prevents us from doing something we really want to do. Describe a time when you became ill and missed out on doing something you'd really been looking forward to.

Sample 6 Score

I'd been looking forward to my 12th birthday for months. We were going to have a party in school and a party at my house after school. My relatives from Ohio were coming, my mom was going to bake my favorite cake, and my brother and his friends were going to DJ. I spent weeks making up the play list, though I might as well have just handed over my pile of Beach Boys albums, because just about every song I chose was a Beach Boys tune. I was the biggest Beach Boys fan on the East coast.

The day before my birthday, however, I came down with the chicken pox. Everything for the next day was cancelled, and I stayed home from school, itchy and cranky. I refused to get out of my pajamas or be civil to anyone. I just sat in my room, playing my Beach Boys albums and feeling miserable. The next day, my birthday, I was still itchy and cranky as can be, a total wretch. Until HE called.

Just after lunch and my third "Three Stooges" episode, the phone rang. It was my dad telling me I had to believe his next statement. I rolled my eyes but agreed.

"In a few minutes, Brian Wilson is going to call you," he said.

"That's not funny, Dad," I replied.

He assured me that it would happen and hung up. He told me I had to believe him and to answer the phone when it rang.

Was he playing a joke on me? No, he couldn't be. My dad knew how much I loved the Beach Boys, and to play a joke of this sort would be too cruel. *He must be serious*, I thought, but I couldn't believe it.

"Okay," I said to myself as I placed the receiver down. *The* Brian Wilson was going to call me? I sat in a daze. Then, before I had a chance to digest what my father said, the phone rang. I thought it was my dad calling back to say he was just teasing. It wasn't.

At the other end of the line was none other than the Brian Wilson. I don't really remember what he said beyond that; once I realized it really was Brian Wilson, I went into a mild state of shock. He must have thought I was a terrible conversationalist because I could only say "yeah" or "no" to most of his questions. After a few minutes, he said goodbye. I hung up the phone, screamed, and cried.

Sample 4 Score

When I was about to turn 12, I came down with the chicken pox. That ruined all of my plans, we were going to have a party in school and a party at my house afterwards. I had all the music picked out that my brother was going to play (DJ) and my mom was making my favorite cake, but, everything got cancelled.

I was miserable as could be. My dad said he'd never seen me be crankier before in his life. I guess that's why he did what he did. He ended up giving me the best birthday present ever.

I think I must have been the biggest Beach Boys fan on the east coast of the United States. I had every record and knew every song. On my birthday, when I was home feeling blue, the phone rang. It was my dad, and he told me that "I have to believe him" and that Brian Wilson, THE Brian Wilson, was going to call me. I couldn't believe it.

"Are you kidding me," I asked my dad?

"No. Please believe me," he answered.

A minute later, the phone rang. "Hello, is Cassandra there," a familiar voice asked. It really was Brian Wilson! He wished me a "Happy Birthday" and told me, "Me and the boys are recording an album here in Indiana." We talked for a few minutes. Or, rather, he talked, and I stuttered, I was so excited and nervous I couldn't hardly say anything.

My dad told me that he managed to track the Beach Boys down and that Brian Wilson heard my story, that I was sick and a big fan on my birthday, and he agreed to call me. What a wonderful thing dad did for me. He made my birthday unforgettable.

Sample 1 Score

Many things can interfere with our plans. Sometime an illness prevents us from something we really want to do. One time I became ill and missed out on something I'd really been looking forward. We cancel my birthday party plan because I have the chicken pocks. I felt really sad. I was 12. I really love the beach boys music and suddenly when I am home crying Brian Wilson, he calls me. I cannot believe!! It was so important. I am so lucky for my dad to do such a thing.

325. Many of our fondest memories are associated with food. Describe a memorable experience that took place while preparing or eating food.

Sample 6 Score

Back when I was in junior high school, all students—boys as well as girls—were required to take home economics. In the fall, we sewed duffel bags and pillows shaped like animals. In the spring, we learned how to cook.

For our final cooking class project, we had to cook a dish at home and bring it to class. I knew right away what I was going to make: my Aunt Rosie's famous chocolate cake.

My aunt Rosie made the best chocolate cake in the world. It was a recipe she had gotten from her grandmother, who swore her grandmother had personally made that chocolate cake for the Prince of Wales. When I started the cooking class, I had asked Aunt Rosie what made her chocolate cake so special. She told me the secret ingredient was coffee.

I had never tried to bake a cake from scratch before, and since the chocolate cake was Aunt Rosie's specialty, I thought for sure she would help me make it.

"But that would be cheating," she said as a she handed me the recipe. "You go home and you make it yourself. Make sure you save a piece for me!" she hollered as I headed out the door.

At home, I got out my ingredients: eggs, butter, milk, sugar, fine powdered chocolate, cinnamon, baking powder, and coffee. The recipe looked easy enough, and I followed each step carefully. When I had mixed everything together, I carefully poured the batter into the pan. I put the cake into the oven, which I had preheated as directed, and set a timer for 50 minutes. When the buzzer went off, I stuck a toothpick into the middle of the cake to make sure it was done. It was perfect.

When the cake cooled, I opened up a can of Betty Crocker's chocolate frosting, spread a thick layer on top of the cake, and covered it with plastic wrap. It was a masterpiece, and I couldn't wait for my classmates to taste it.

The next morning, I carried my cake carefully to school. I passed out pieces to my classmates, beaming with pride. But when I saw the look on their faces, I knew something was terribly wrong. I took a bite and nearly burst into tears. No wonder they looked disgusted! Aunt Rosie's cake was never crunchy, and the crunchy things were bitter. The cake tasted awful. My heart sank as I watched Mrs. Wilson take a bite. She crunched, paused, crunched again, paused again, and looked at me thoughtfully.

"Sarah," she said gently, "does the recipe for this cake call for coffee?"

"Yes," I replied.

"Hmmm. I thought so."

When I questioned her about my mistake, she said, "You used coffee *grounds*. You were supposed to use *liquid* coffee," she said, and she laughed gently.

I was mortified. I vowed to correct my mistake and make a new cake for tomorrow.

This time, with a real cup of coffee, I baked a cake that would have made Aunt Rosie proud.

Sample 4 Score

One of my most memorable school experiences had to do with food preparation. I was making a cake for my cooking class in junior high school, but things didn't turn out the way I'd planned.

We all had to make something at home for our final cooking project, and I wanted to make my Aunt Rosie's famous chocolate cake. She made the best chocolate cake in the world, all of my family and friends agreed. It was an easy enough recipe, I thought. What made it different—better than— most chocolate cakes was its secret ingredient, coffee.

When I had all of the ingredients out I started making the cake. I followed the recipe exactly, putting in three-quarters cup of coffee, just like the recipe called for. I put it in the oven at precisely 350 degrees and cooked it for exactly one hour. When I took it out of the oven, it looked beautiful. I covered it with some chocolate frosting and set it aside to take to school in the morning. I was so proud of it!

When I got to cooking class, however, I realized something was wrong. People made funny faces when they bit into the cake. So I tried it too, and it tasted awful. It was bitter and crunchy. Aunt Rosie's cake never tasted like this! What did I do wrong?

My teacher asked me if the recipe called for coffee. Yes, I told her. "You used coffee grounds, didn't you," she asked.

"Yes," I answered.

That was my mistake. I was supposed to use brewed coffee, not coffee grounds. Mrs. Wilson was really nice, though; she allowed me to make another cake for the next class and bring it in. That time, I did it right. My cake was delicious. It would have made Aunt Rosie proud!

Sample 1 Score

I like to cook. In school I even had a cooking class. We learn everything from measuring to whats different from frying and baking. The school was a nice kitchen for practicing. My friend Alisha was the best cook. She and her whole family cooked. In my family Aunt Rosie is the best cook. One time I baked a cake for class, and I messed it up bad and everyone in class though it was nasty tasting. I did it again the next time and it was delicious. Even Aunt Rosie think so.

341.   Try as we might to avoid them, accidents happen. Tell about a time when you were involved in an accident.

Sample 6 Score

I was never one to believe in things like miracles or fate, but since my accident a few months ago, I look at things a little differently. Whether it was a miracle, or fate, or just plain luck, I'm still here to tell this story.

It was a Monday morning, just about 8:15. I was actually a little early for once and was glad I didn't have to race to work. It was my second week as a bank teller at Harrison Savings and Loan.

There had been some freezing rain earlier that morning, but the roads seemed clear as I pulled out of the driveway. I turned left at the light, right at the Dunkin Donuts, and then left again onto the onramp for Route 61. I sped up to merge with the oncoming rush-hour traffic when suddenly I felt my car, a brand new Durango, lose control. I'd hit a patch of ice.

What happened next probably lasted no more than fifteen seconds, but if felt like hours. I spun around like a top, turning two full revolutions as I crossed the two southbound lanes. Then I hit the median strip and the car flipped over as it crossed into the northbound traffic. I skidded across the highway and the car stopped in the right-hand lane. There I was, upside-down and backwards, after crashing across four lanes, and somehow I was alive. Somehow I hadn't hit a single car.

But I had no time to appreciate that miracle, because when I looked out the shattered windshield, I saw an 18-wheeler was bearing down upon me at about 65 miles an hour. There was no time to get out of the car.

I screamed and braced myself for the impact. But instead of hearing the crunch of metal crashing into metal, I heard the screeching of brakes as the truck swerved around me, just in time to avoid a head-on collision. The truck skidded to a stop on the shoulder about a hundred feet away from me. Then the driver jumped out and ran over to see if I was okay.

That night at home, I eased my aching body into bed. But I was climbing into my own bed, in my own room, not in the hospital. Somehow, the only injuries I sustained were a few cuts on my face and hands, a bruised right shoulder, and two bruised calf muscles. My new car was totaled, but I didn't care. All that mattered was that I was alive.

Sample 4 Score

I was involved in a really terrible accident not long ago, and I'm very lucky to be alive. I was on my way to work at my new job when I hit a patch of ice as I was pulling onto a major highway. It's a miracle I didn't get seriously hurt.

When I hit the patch of ice, my car, my brand new Durango, that I was so proud of, lost control. I started spinning around like a top. I spun across the two north-bound lanes. Then my car hit the median strip and flipped over.

I thought, I ought to be dead already, but I wasn't. But it wasn't over yet. Now I went across the south bound lanes upsidedown. I stopped in the right hand lane and then I saw a big truck headed straight towards me.

Somehow, I don't know how, that truck managed to stop before it crashed into me. It swerved around me and saved my life. Then the driver got out to see if I was ok.

Luckily, I was OK. I only had just a few cuts and bruises and I bruised both of my calf muscles. My car was totaled, but, that didn't matter. I was just happy to be alive.

Sample 1 Score

One time I had bad accident. That almost got me killed. I hit a pach of ice. When I was go onto high way I spinned around a lot. Across all for lanes. First I hit the midean stripe that made my car flipped over. I was upside down thanking I was still a live. When a big truck was coming at me. There wasnt no time to got out. It was my brand new car that was totalled. I was ok after all that lucky for me my car wrecked but not me. The truck he stop on time and move around my car upsidedown still. He jump to see if I ok.

In hospital doctors say I ok. Just many number of bruises and cuts and some on my calfs and shoulder. I am ok all thogh my car it ruined.

342. Describe an experience you had that would be considered a near miss or a brush with disaster.

Sample 6 Score

I must have had a guardian angel that day.

I was six and had just learned how to ride a bicycle. My bike was a beauty: pink all over, with a stylish banana seat, iridescent fringes hanging off the handle bars, and a white woven basket with big, pink flowers on the front.

It was a Monday afternoon and I was alone, riding my bike in circles in the driveway. I was exalting in my freedom: no more training wheels, no more big brother or father pushing me from behind and holding me steady. Now I could start, stop, and ride all by myself, and I went around and around our circular driveway in complete bliss.

The sun shone on my face and made the black pavement hot, even though it was already late September. Emboldened by the warmth of the sun and the excitement of my success—eight laps around and I hadn't fallen yet—I decided it was time to leave the safety of the circle and ride down the steep hill that led to the road on which we lived: Route 309, a four-lane, heavily-traveled highway. I warmed up with another two or three turns around the circle and then eased to my right and down the slope.

From the start of the circle to the edge of the highway, the driveway ran about 200 feet at an even 45 degrees. I began to pick up a lot of speed at 50 feet, more at 75, and by 100 feet I was flying. The road was getting closer; I could see the faces of the people driving by at 50, 60, 70 miles an hour. It was time to slow down, but I couldn't. I kept going faster, and faster, and I couldn't stop. In my panic, I forgot how to use the brakes.

In an instant I was out on the highway, a little pink streak that zoomed across all four lanes and somehow, someway, ended up on the other side, up on the Zeigler's lawn, in one piece. In the seconds that it took me to cross the road, there had not been a single car. An instant later, they were back, and I had to wait several minutes before I slowly, shakily, walked my bike back across the street and up the driveway.

I never told anyone about what happened, and it was a long, long time before I ventured down that slope again. When I did, I used my brakes the whole way down. This time, I wasn't going to forget.

Sample 4 Score

I once had a brush with disaster and nearly got myself killed. I was six and just learned how to ride my bike by myself. I loved my bike. It was pink and had a banana seat and a basket in front.

On the day that this happened, I was riding around in our driveway. Our driveway was a long hill and then a big circle at the top. I was riding around in the circle.

It was the first time I was all alone on my bike. After a while because I didn't fall at all, I decided to go down the hill. I start down the slope and I realize I can't remember how to break. This of course is a problem because I start going faster and faster, any minute I will be out on the highway.

We lived on Route 309, a 4-lane highway that was always busy with cars. Suddenly I was zooming across that road. Somehow, I made it across all four lanes without getting hit by a car.

I don't know how I was so lucky, to not be hurt at all that day. Because a minute later, as soon as I was across, there were more cars on the road than I could count. Somehow, when I was going across, there just weren't any cars. Maybe I had a guardian angel watching over me.

Sample 1 Score

When I have just learned to ride a bike, I almost have a big accident. That almost gets me killed. My favorite bike, I'm riding it around and around in the driveway. I like this bike so much. My aunt, she gived it to me as a present. For my birthday.

All of a suddenly I am starting going down the hill, I forgot how to stop, I am going across the road. There are four lanes and lots of cars. Somehow I don't get hit by nothing. I walk my bike back up the hill. I am thinking never to tell anyone. Boy I am so lucky!

359. We all need help from others from time to time. Tell about a time you helped someone in need.

Sample 6 Score

It was the hottest day of the summer, a record-breaking 102 degrees, hot and humid, sweltering even in the shade. I was driving back from visiting my older brother and his new baby. In the blistering heat, I could see the blacktop bubbling. I'd never been so grateful for air conditioning before.

I cruised happily along County Route 2, which wound through the northern tip of the Sonoran Desert. Then I saw that a car had broken down up ahead. It was the first car I'd seen in about half an hour. In the distance, a few hundred feet ahead of the car, I saw a stooped figure walking with a gas can in his hands. There was nothing around for miles. There was no way this person was going to make it to the nearest town, which was a good twenty miles away, in this desert heat.

I'd always been told to stay away from strangers, but I thought if there ever was a time to do a good deed, this was it. Besides, as I neared the figure, I could tell that it was an elderly man, and I thought there was little chance he'd do me any harm. So I slowed down and pulled over. "Need a lift?" I asked.

Now that I could see him clearly, it was obvious the old man was already in trouble. He'd only walked a hundred yards or so, and he looked as if he was going to pass out any moment. "I'd be most grateful, young lady, if you could help me get to a gas station," he said slowly. "I seem to be out of petroleum."

"No problem," I replied. "I'm headed that way."

He climbed slowly into the car and I pulled back out onto the road. "Not a good day for car trouble, huh?" I asked.

"Indeed," he replied. He was silent for a few minutes while his body temperature normalized. I offered him a soda from the cooler I'd packed for my four-hour ride. He accepted it gratefully. We made a little small talk then, but just a little. He seemed to prefer the silence.

As we neared the gas station, I asked him if he would like a ride back to his car. "I don't have to be home until late this afternoon," I told him. "It's no trouble."

"I know it is quite out of your way," he replied. "I would be most grateful." He paused. "And just where is home, young lady?"

"Elmwood," I replied.

I introduced myself as Emily Hampton and found out that he was Edward Gilliam. "By the way, my name is Emily. Emily Hampton."

"You're a very kind lady, Ms. Hampton. My name is Edward Gilliam."

Edward filled up his gas can and I drove him back to his car. We filled up his tank, and I followed him back into town just to make sure he was ok. At the gas station, I beeped and waved and continued north towards home. Edward waved and nodded his thanks.

The next morning, the doorbell rang. My mom answered. "Emily!" she hollered. "Get down here!" I came down the stairs and saw a giant bouquet of flowers. They were stunning. A small note was attached:

"Dearest Emily, thank you for your incredible kindness yesterday. You just might have saved my life, and I am eternally grateful. You reminded an old man of how much beauty there is in this world. Yours, Edward Gilliam."

Sample 4 Score

I'd never picked up a hitchhiker or helped anyone along the highway before that day. But with that heat, how could I just drive by. It was the hottest day ever, I was driving through the desert when I passed a broken-down car. An old man was walking along the road carrying a gas can, I had to stop.

I asked him if he needed a ride. Which was a silly question—of course he did. It was over 100 degrees and the nearest town was more than 20 miles away. He'd die before he made it five miles in those conditions.

We didn't talk much; I think he was the quiet type. I offered him a soda and he drank it down like that. When we got to the nearest gas station, I asked him, if he wanted me to drive him back to his car? "It won't be any trouble," I told him. I didn't have to be home until the end of the day.

So we filled up his gas can and I drove him back. We talked a little more this time. He asked where I lived, and he told me he was on his way to visit his granddaughter. We filled up his tank and I followed him for a while to make sure he was ok. Then I drove the rest of the way home.

Next morning, the doorbell rang, there was a huge boquet of flowers for me. They were from Edward (that was his name). He was very grateful; he said "I saved his life yesterday" and that "I reminded him there was so much beauty in the world." I was so glad that I helped him.

Sample 1 Score

Everyone needs help sometime. One day I help an old man who car break down on the road in the hot hot dessert. He need a ride to get gas. He was so thankful he sends me a big giant bunch of flowers the next day.

Their was never such a hot day, he was crazy to try walking to get gas, the gas station was so far away. It was a dessert so their wasn't no shade or anything or places to rest awhile. He would have been in trouble for sure if I don't help. At the gas station I tell him I can take him back to his car, its not any problem because I have all day. His so thankful to me.

Literary Response Prompts

Choose one of the literary response prompts from the list below and write an essay. A certain number of prompts have model essays in the answer section that you can use to compare and contrast your writing. A scoring guide or rubric is also included in the answer section. You can use this guide to give you an idea of the way your essay may be graded. If you have trouble interpreting the scoring guide, see a teacher or professor for help. Sample responses to the prompts in bold can be found at the end of the section.

377. **Tone is the mood or feeling the author intends the reader to experience. Using a specific piece of literature, explain how tone enhances the work.**

378. Poetry has been defined as, "putting the best possible words in the best possible order." Explain what this means and apply this theory to a specific poem.

379. American Beat generation poet Jack Kerouac has embraced other religions and non-western philosophies that can be evidenced in his work. Explain/discuss how this is apparent to his readers. Use specific evidence in your answer.

380. Often in literature, there is a heroic figure, or archetype. Discuss the characteristics of an *archetype*, using specific examples from a piece of literature.

381. **In the novel, *The Lord of the Flies*, by William Golding, a group of boys are stranded on a remote island to fend for themselves. Compare/contrast this novel to the popular television show *Survivor*. Use specific details in your answer.**

382. The poet Emily Dickinson once said that her sensitivity was comparable to missing a layer of skin. Explain how this analogy is reflected in her poetry.

383. **Using a specific literary work, explain how a novel might influence change in society.**

384. **The theme of a literary piece is the central idea or message that it delivers. Cite a specific literary work and discuss the theme.**

385. Anne Frank became famous for keeping a diary during her experiences in the Holocaust. Explain how simply keeping a diary gave Anne such worldwide recognition.

386. Write a lengthy, detailed journal entry from the point of view of someone you have studied in history. Include accurate, historical details in the diary entry.

387. **Compare/contrast the fear of terrorism and the concern with safety issues in present day society with George Orwell's novel, *1984*.**

388. A haiku is a three-line, non-rhyming poem usually centered on nature. It has also been defined as a snapshot of something ordinary. From your own experience, describe the natural images you feel are worthy of a haiku.

389. A struggle between two or more opposing forces in a work is called conflict. Cite a piece of literature and explain the conflict embodied in the work.

390. Personification is the technique wherein a non-human character is given human thoughts, feelings, and dialogue. Illustrate how this technique is used in your favorite novel or short story.

391. Walt Whitman uses second-person narration—a technique not often used by writers—in his poem *Crossing Brooklyn Ferry*. In second person narration, the narrator speaks directly to you. Discuss another work that uses second person narration. Give examples from the work.

392. The setting of a novel is where the action takes place. Explain how the setting complements the story in a novel you have read.

393. The climax of a work is when all of the events come to a breaking point. Using a piece of literature that you know, explain the events that lead to the climax, what happens at the climactic scene, and how the story changes after the climax.

394. Third person point of view is when the narrator has no part in the action. He or she is simply telling the story using the words *he*, *she*, or *they*. A story would be very different if it were told from the first person (using the pronoun *I*) point of view. Using a novel written in the third person, discuss how it would be a very different story if it were told in the first person.

395. Many times in Shakespeare's plays, the setting changes from rural or pastoral to urban. Compare and contrast these settings. Explain the reason for the shift of scenery, using support from specific plays.

396. Describe the plot of a novel that would portray the attitudes and feelings of the people and the society in the year 2002.

397. List ten sensory images for each of the four seasons—winter, spring, summer, and fall. Then, write a brief explanation of why you chose those specific images.

398. Narrative poetry tells a story and doesn't necessarily rhyme. Often, narrative poems are written about historical events. Name three historical events that could be considered worthy of a narrative poem. Describe the key elements from each historical event.

399. Describe a character from literature that you would trade places with, and explain why.

400. Imagine that you could become an omniscient character in a literary piece and change the plot somehow. Describe the piece of literature in which the character belongs, and tell how that character would alter the plot. Use details from the literary piece that you have chosen.

401. Explain the popularity of science fiction writing. Use a work from this genre to explain its appeal.

402. Using a work of literature you have read, describe the hero or heroine and his or her characteristics.

403. The protagonist in a story is usually the do-gooder, or the character that most readers emphathize with. Identify a piece of literature where the author wants us to empathize with the antagonist, or evildoer. Explain by using details from that work.

404. In drama, when a character speaks his or her innermost thoughts, it is called a monologue. Explain your favorite monologue from a dramatic piece and tell how this monologue affected the plot.

405. Explain the appeal of war literature. Use a piece of literature from this genre to describe its allure.

406. Foreshadowing is when the author gives hints to the reader about what is going to take place later in the work. Using a piece of literature that you are familiar with, explain how the author uses foreshadowing and how the use of foreshadowing added to the plot.

407. Novels such as John Steinbeck's *The Winter of Our Discontent* and Ernest Hemingway's *For Whom the Bell Tolls* take their titles from lines in Shakespearean plays. Write an essay explaining and interpreting the significance of one of these titles and how it captures the theme of the book.

408. Discuss a character in literature that you loathed. Explain the techniques the author used that caused you to feel this way.

409. In William Faulkner's *Barn Burning*, a young boy must decide whether to turn his father in for breaking the law, or to stay loyal to his family. Write about a situation in real life that is similar to this one.

410. Conflict, in a work of literature, is the struggle between opposing characters or opposing forces. One type of conflict is character vs. character. Explain this type of conflict using a piece of literature that you have read.

411. Another type of conflict is called character vs. nature. Using a piece of literature that you are familiar with, explain how the author uses this type of conflict.

412. **A third type of conflict is called character vs. him/herself. This is also referred to as internal conflict, because the character must face self-inflicted fears and problems. Write about this type of conflict, using a piece of literature that you have read.**

413. Discuss the key events that you would offer to a person writing a biography of your life.

414. Novels often become mirror images of life. Discuss a time when you saw a similarity between your life and that of the main character in a novel. Explain the situation and compare the way you handled the situation with the way the character did.

415. Explain the most important lesson you learned from a piece of literature. Use specific details from a literary work you have read.

416. **Discuss a piece of literature in which the author is also the narrator. Describe the way he or she uses actual events from his or her life in his or her writing.**

417. Oral tradition is a form of storytelling that is passed on from generation to generation. It has often been said that an original story could be altered from when it is first told to when it was first written. Give examples of how this could happen using evidence from a story you know in the oral tradition.

418. Explain the items you would want to place in a time capsule.

419. Flashback is a technique whereby past events are recalled while telling a story in the present. Discuss this technique as it was used in a piece of literature that you have read and tell why this was the best way to tell the story.

420. Discuss your favorite character from Greek mythology. Be sure to include details and elements from the myth as you describe this character.

421. Repetition is a technique used by a poet to create sound or to emphasize a subject in a poem. Discuss how and why this technique is used in a poem that you know.

422. Discuss whether or not a piece of literature has ever predicted actual events. Using a work that you are familiar with, discuss this topic using specific details.

423. Ralph Waldo Emerson once wrote in one of his essays that he thought it amusing when a man could wear an expensive wristwatch, but could not tell time by looking at the position of the sun in the sky. Explain what he is saying about modern people and society.

424. Often, in literature, a character is viewed as an outsider or a loner. Using a piece of literature that you are familiar with, discuss such a character. Be sure to describe this character's attitudes towards himself or herself, and how he or she deals with the isolation that comes with these two labels.

425. Discuss a character from literature that seems to be present only for comic relief. Explain how this character adds to or detracts from the work.

426. Death has been symbolized many different ways in prose and poetry. Using either of these genres, discuss the symbols that authors use when they write about death. Describe the impact of these symbols.

427. Often, an author will give the reader more information than the characters have. Using a piece of literature that you are familiar with, speculate on the reasons an author would use this method.

428. Sometimes an author will write dialogue that illustrates a person's intelligence, speech pattern, or locality. Discuss a piece of literature in which this happens. Also discuss whether this technique helps or hinders your reading.

429. Discuss a piece of literature that uses the theme of personal survival.

430. Frequently, popular novels are adapted into motion pictures. Discuss a novel that you have read and that has been made into a motion picture. Compare/contrast the plot, setting, and characterization in both mediums.

431. The *coming of age* theme is very popular in literature. This term refers to a pre-adolescent boy or girl going through many difficult, life altering experiences in order to reach young adulthood. Using a novel you are familiar with, discuss this theme. Be sure to use supporting details and evidence in your essay.

432. Shakespeare's tragedy *Romeo and Juliet* is a powerful drama about young love and familial conflict. Compare this play to another piece of literature that you have read and that embodies the same themes.

433. Discuss the themes of two fairy tales that you know. Tell how these themes benefit young children.

434. Imagery is the use of descriptive details that appeal to the reader's senses. Using a literary piece that you are familiar with, discuss how the author's use of imagery enhanced your reading experience.

435. Compare how a social studies textbook and historical fiction are similar yet different. Explain which medium you would want to choose in order to learn more about a historical period.

436. Each culture has its own unique literature. Discuss the literary contributions made by one particular culture. Cite a least three major works to illustrate your point.

437. Music and poetry have many similarities. Discuss the connection using specific examples from both musical and poetic works.

438. In the beginning of a novel, an author may present a character one way, but by the end of the novel, this same character may behave differently. Through characterization, we can learn to understand people. Using a piece of literature that you have read, discuss the ways in which the author used characterization to present personality.

439. Explore the theme of social breakdown or anarchy, using a piece of literature that you have read.

440. Explore the theme of personal degeneration and abandoning morals, using a piece of literature that you have read.

441. Discuss the theme of social injustice, using a piece of literature that you have read.

442. Discuss a piece of literature in which the setting switches between the past and the present.

443. Discuss a literary trilogy wherein the reader must read the succession of novels to understand the plot.

444. Discuss a specific literary work that focuses on adolescent main characters.

445. Discuss how faith is symbolized in a piece of literature that you have read.

446. A burlesque, such as Oscar Wilde's *The Importance of Being Earnest*, is a literary piece that explores a serious subject in a trivial manner or a trivial subject in a serious manner. Choose a literary work that fits this description and explain why it should be classified as a burlesque.

447. Discuss how the reader might sympathize with the main character in Christopher Marlowe's *Dr. Faustus*, even though he sells his soul to the Devil.

448. Discuss the theme of prejudice, using a piece of literature that you have read.

449. Discuss a piece of literature that you had to read more than once in order to fully understand it. Explain how and why the meaning of the piece became more clear to you.

450. Using a literary piece that you are familiar with, discuss a character who begins as a minor character, but who evolves into a major character with an important role as the novel progresses.

451. Discuss a piece of literature that uses an object of worth, such as a sword, as its focus. Discuss the symbolic purpose of this object.

452. Discuss the imagery from a Civil War period novel that you have read.

453. **Discuss a hero in a literary piece that you have read.**

454. Using a piece of literature that you are familiar with, discuss the theme of unrequited love.

455. Discuss why Shakespeare used only men and boys in his dramatic works at the Globe Theater.

456. Using a piece of literature that you are familiar with, discuss how one character influences other characters to change.

457. Discuss a piece of literature that utilizes spirits or ghosts.

458. Discuss a character from literature that embodies a dark mood.

459. Discuss your favorite historical poem, its theme, and the historical events on which the poem is based.

460. Discuss the use of metaphor, imagery, and word play in Lewis Carroll's *Alice in Wonderland.*

461. Discuss an immigrant's point of view in America, using a piece of literature that you have read.

462. Discuss the theme of greed in a piece of literature that you have read.

463. Discuss a prominent leader in our society and his or her literary influences. Discuss what this reveals about that leader.

464. Discuss a piece of literature from the Industrial Revolution and its treatment of issues like child labor, working conditions, and social classes.

465. Write a literary analysis of a Robert Frost poem. Include theme and symbolism in your discussion.

466. Discuss the effect and significance of Maya Angelou's poetry reading at Bill Clinton's inauguration.

467. Analyze a poem that uses a pessimistic tone.

468. Analyze a poem that uses a hopeful, optimistic tone.

469. Discuss a figure from history, other than Anne Frank, whose journal entries have spawned a classic literary piece.

470. Often in literature, a character has ironic experiences that can be humorous or fateful. Discuss how this technique was used in a piece of literature that you have read.

471. Discuss a piece of literature set in another country, and how this venue enhanced your enjoyment of the piece.

472. Compare the character Holden Caulfield from J.D. Salinger's *Catcher in the Rye* to someone you know.

473. Analyze a literary work from the Harlem Renaissance.

474. Using a piece of literature that you are familiar with, discuss the theme of personal suffering and loss.

475. Using a piece of literature that you are familiar with, discuss the theme of personal triumph.

476. Using a piece of literature that you have read, discuss the way your views about another culture were changed.

477. Using a piece of literature that you have read, discuss how fate intervened and came to the aid of a character.

478. Discuss your favorite story from Roman mythology.

479. Using a piece of literature that you are familiar with, discuss a character who served as a guide, and explain that character's purpose.

480. Discuss how irony helped a character in a dramatic work that you have read.

481. Compare a contemporary piece of literature with an older piece that contains the same theme.

482. Discuss a piece of literature with which you are familiar that centers on a physical journey.

483. Compare the society of *The Scarlet Letter* to our society today. Compare and contrast how Hester Prynne would have been treated today with how she was treated in the novel.

484. Discuss the theme of nature in a piece of literature that you have read.

485. Discuss a character who goes through a complete mental breakdown, using a piece of literature that you are familiar with.

486. Discuss why the *Harry Potter* series is so popular with readers.

487. Using a piece of literature that you are familiar with, discuss a determined main character.

488. Using a piece of literature that you are familiar with, discuss how the weather or climate affects the mood or tone.

489. Discuss how technology plays a major role in a literary work that you have read.

490. Using a piece of literature that you are familiar with, discuss how struggle is symbolized.

491. Using a piece of literature that you are familiar with, discuss how evil is personified.

492. Discuss a well-known piece of literature that contains a mythical beast.

493. Using your knowledge of contemporary writers, speculate as to who might become the next literary giant.

494. Discuss a novel that you think might be the best novel of the twentieth century.

495. Discuss someone from literature whose name is indicative of their character. An example might be Willy Loman (or Lo-man) from Arthur Miller's *Death of A Salesman*.

496. Discuss how doom is foreshadowed in a piece of literature that you are familiar with.

497. Discuss the difference between poetry and prose, using literary pieces that you have read.

498. Discuss a novel that has been controversial and perhaps banned, and explain why.

499. Discuss the complicated relationship between Lenny and George in John Steinbeck's *Of Mice and Men*.

500. An allegory is a literary piece in which the surface plot, characters, and theme convey a symbolic meaning. Discuss the use of allegory in George Orwell's *Animal Farm*.

501. Discuss a poem that you think might be used as the keynote speech for a meeting at the United Nations.

RUBRIC FOR LITERARY RESPONSE WRITING

Score	6	5	4	3	2	1
	For a grade at this level, your writing:	For a grade at this level, your writing:	For a grade at this level, your writing:	For a grade at this level, your writing:	For a grade at this level, your writing:	For a grade at this level, your writing:
Content: Your written response shows an understanding and interpretation of the writing prompt.	■ satisfies the requirements of the writing prompt in a creative and original manner. ■ establishes a controlling idea that reveals an understanding of the text. ■ uses a clear thesis statement. ■ proves the thesis with insightful examples and details.	■ provides a thoughtful analysis of the writing prompt. ■ establishes a controlling idea that reveals a complete understanding of the text. ■ provides a clear thesis statement. ■ offers good examples to confirm the thesis statement.	■ meets some of the requirements of the writing prompt. ■ establishes a controlling idea that shows a basic understanding of the text. ■ includes some key elements that help explain the thesis.	■ offers a simple interpretation of the writing prompt. ■ makes an attempt to establish a controlling idea, but it is weak. ■ makes superficial connections between the controlling idea and the text.	■ meets few of the requirements of the writing prompt. ■ reveals an incomplete understanding of the text. ■ fails to establish a controlling idea. ■ gives no examples to help explain the thesis.	■ minimally addresses the writing prompt. ■ reveals a minimal understanding of the text. ■ makes no connection to the text, to the ideas in the text, or to literary elements in the text.
Development: Your written response gives a clear and logical explanation of ideas, using supporting material.	■ builds and elaborates ideas thoroughly. ■ uses examples precisely. ■ develops the topic in an interesting and imaginative way. ■ demonstrates coherence in the development of ideas	■ develops the topic in an acceptable way. ■ uses relevant examples throughout the essay. ■ develops ideas clearly and consistently.	■ responds to some ideas more completely than others. ■ uses some specific and relevant evidence from the text.	■ shows weakness in the development of ideas and/or develops ideas without thorough explanation.	■ contains inaccurate, vague, or repetitive details. ■ has limited development of ideas.	■ shows a lack of development of ideas.
Organization: Your written response shows a coherent, orderly, well-reasoned approach.	■ sets up and maintains a clear focus based on the controlling idea. ■ establishes a logical, rational sequence of ideas with transitional words and sentences.	■ maintains focus on the controlling idea. ■ has an obvious plan of organization. ■ uses appropriate devices and transitions.	■ has a general focus. ■ obviously attempts organization but lacks consistency.	■ does not show a logical sense of organization. ■ strays from the topic. ■ can be difficult to follow.	■ suggests some organization but lacks focus.	■ exhibits no organizational pattern or focus.
Language Use/ Conventions: Your written response shows a sense of audience by using effective vocabulary and varied sentence structure.	■ has vivid language, fluidity, and a sense of engagement and voice. ■ has sophisticated style of sentence structure, sentence variety, and vocabulary. ■ has essentially no errors.	■ has good control of mechanics. ■ contains some errors when using sophisticated language. ■ has a slightly lower quality of sentence structure and sentence variety. ■ shows errors when using sophisticated vocabulary only.	■ has a sense of audience. ■ uses simple sentences. ■ uses an appropriate level of vocabulary. ■ demonstrates partial control of mechanics. ■ exhibits some errors that do not interfere with comprehension.	■ uses vocabulary that is slightly below level. ■ has a vague sense of audience. ■ shows a beginner's control of the language. ■ has errors that begin to interfere with comprehension.	■ exhibits little control of the language. ■ has errors that make comprehension difficult	■ shows minimal control of language skills. ■ may be illegible or unrecognizable as English.

A ZERO PAPER is:
■ totally unrelated to the topic.
■ filled with indecipherable words and is illegible.
■ incoherent with illogical or garbled syntax.
■ blank.

Scoring Explanations for Literary Response Essays

A score of "**6**" indicates that your essay satisfies the requirements of the writing prompt in a creative and original manner, using an obvious theme and thesis throughout. The essay provides a clear and logical explanation of your ideas, using specific support material, including direct quotations from the literary work. You thoroughly articulate your ideas in a coherent fashion, analyze and interpret specific literary elements and concepts, and avoid simple plot summary. The essay is orderly and well reasoned, with a clear focus, a logical sequence of ideas, and transitional words and sentences. The essay demonstrates a sense of audience by using effective vocabulary, varied sentence structure, and fluid, sophisticated language that is essentially without errors.

A score of "**4**" indicates that your essay meets some of the requirements of the writing prompt, including some key elements that help explain the thesis. The essay may answer the question in an abbreviated manner or rely heavily on plot summary, giving only brief or general examples and developing ideas somewhat inconsistently. Literary elements and concepts may only be minimally addressed. You give the essay a general focus, make an obvious attempt at organization, and present your ideas in a logical sequence. The language of the essay indicates a general control of mechanics but has a slightly lower quality of sentence structure and variety than a sample 6 score. An essay of this type contains errors only when using sophisticated language.

A score of "**1**" indicates that your essay only minimally addresses the writing prompt, digressing, repeating, or dwelling on insignificant details throughout. The essay shows a lack of development and exhibits no organizational pattern or focus. Your language skills may be illegible or unrecognizable as English.

Model Literary Response Essays

377. Tone is the mood or feeling the author intends the reader to experience. Using a specific piece of literature, explain how tone enhances the work.

Sample 6 Score

Writers for TV sitcoms or movies are fortunate. Visuals often convey tone much more conveniently than words. Writers have to be very skillful in word choice in order to evoke emotions. While I began to explore Edgar Allan Poe's works, I was intrigued with the way Poe carefully chose language and with the way it evoked a very certain mood or tone.

In Poe's "The Tell-Tale Heart", I was amazed with the way the main character could grow to hate someone's physical appearance so much so that he could stare at him for hours on end. The plot of this story revolves around a young man who rents a room from an elderly man in a large, dark mansion. This is how Poe begins to create the tone or mood. If the setting were in a house with a white picket fence in Pleasantville, the setting might not be as effective for suspense or horror. However, Poe begins to masterfully build suspense in "The Tell-Tale Heart". For example, the deranged tenant slowly opens the elderly man's bedroom door at night and stares at his glass eye for hours in a seething rage. He does this numerous times, to where the reader begins to understand that this man is far from normal. His obsession leads him to commit a horrible crime.

The rage this man feels about the eye finally comes to a point wherein he attacks the man and suffocates him in his bed. Afterwards, he dismembers his corpse and hides the pieces under the floorboards. By now, the reader is in complete disbelief and awe at such a heinous, non-provoked attack, that we must continue reading. The tone becomes very eerie, and will soon turn suspenseful.

Finally, the police investigate the home after a neighbor reported hearing screams coming from the house. The deranged man invites the police in, and invites them to sit with him in the room where the corpse lies. Poe now adds to the tone with more suspense and a feeling of anxiety to whether the man will confess to the murder. While speaking with the police, the man begins to hear a faint heartbeat that continues to grow in volume. However, he is the only one who hears the noise. The man attempted to cunningly fool the police officers while sitting on the corpse, only to now mentally break down from the noise inside his mind to where he confesses. The torture this man evokes on himself adds tremendously to the tone of the story.

Just as Poe creates an eerie, intense, and twisted tone to his fiction, authors can lead their readers to feel certain emotions through their writing.

Sample 4 Score

Tone can be called the way an author makes you feel while reading their work. I personally have been frightened, brought to tears, extremely angry, and have laughed out loud simply by the way an author creates the tone of a story. This is also very similar to what an audience experiences while watching a film.

I recall one work I read by Edgar Allen Poe called The Telltale Heart, which has a bizarre, twisted tone.

Initially, I thought this story was simply about a man who takes in a stranger. However, the tone of the story became strange when the tenant stares at his landlord while he sleeps. Poe leads us into the mind of a madman. I was on the edge of my seat as the police were asking questions of the man. The tone of the story, or the mood, was both frightening and suspenseful.

I enjoy reading all types of books because many times the tone is different. I especially like Poe's stories because I now know how he used tone in his twisted tales.

Sample 1 Score

Tone is like when the writer makes you feel good when you read books. I like to read a lot. In this essay I will tell you about tone.

I like many books that have tone. If you don't have tone, then sometimes I don't like to read these kinds. I like to read books about animuls, cars, and misteries. I really like misteries because you try an figure out what happens.

In this essay I have told you about tone.

381. In the novel, *The Lord of the Flies*, by William Golding, a group of boys are stranded on a remote island to fend for themselves. Compare/contrast this novel to the popular television show *Survivor*. Use specific details in your answer.

Sample 6 Score

William Golding's novel *The Lord of the Flies* explores many themes such as the dark side of human nature, allegiances, and how these boys mirror larger society. I feel as if the producers of the popular television show "Survivor" used this novel as the framework of their show. Both Golding's novel and the show have many similarities.

When the show "Survivor" premiered, I immediately thought of the novel *The Lord of the Flies*. The novel is about a group of schoolboys who are shipwrecked on a deserted island. The boys attempt to create a "civilization," but ultimately transform into mere savages. This is an important novel for the psychological study Golding presents. One can't help but draw parallels to adult society. There is a true need for structure and control in any society, but the means of that control makes this novel all the more interesting.

One of the boys, Jack, is power-hungry and represents dictatorship. Some of the other boys such as Simon and Piggy try to do what is safe and conservative. The character of Ralph is symbolic of democracy and fairness. Throughout the novel, the boys engage in a power struggle and end up destroying one another. Golding's use of symbolism forces the reader to see characters and situations as larger ideas. The boys realize that they must create some type of order.

Similar to the television show "Survivor", the boys hold council meetings, use objects as a symbol of strength, and use fire as a symbol of hope. I remember watching the show and observing a contestant who won a physical contest against the other players. This person was given a pillow to use, whereas the other contestants had nothing. The pillow symbolizes power, as did the conch in the novel. Also, whenever the show's council met on Sunday nights, they all brought their torches. When someone was voted off the island (seen as a liability or risk to the welfare of the group), that person's torch was extinguished, thus eliminating hope. Alliances were formed and these alliances pitted the contestants against each other. Ultimately the winner was the most cunning player who could convince the other members to follow them. This is exactly the situation that occurred between Ralph and Jack in the novel.

William Golding's novel allows the reader to explore human nature and mankind. Often, we do not like to face the psychological aspects of our being. "Survivor" emulates the same underlying motives that form our nature.

Sample 4 Score

In William Goldings *The Lord of the Flies*, I can draw many parallels between the group of boys in the story and the basis for the television show "Survivor".

In "Survivor", contestants are forced to live together on a deserted island for a prolonged period of time. The rules are to form alliances and not to be deceived by the other players. This is similar to what happens in the novel *The Lord of the Flies*. A group of shipwrecked boys must form a society in order to have structure. Jack and Ralph are the two leaders with totally different ways of order. One wants to be a dictator and the other wants to be democratic.

Another similarity between the novel and the show is that they place importance on objects. In the book, the conch is symbolic of power. On the show, if someone wins a race or something, they get a prize and the others don't have anything! Also, both use fire as a lifeline. In the show, when you are voted off the island, you must put out your torch. And both the show and novel have tribal meetings.

I think the show "Survivor" and *The Lord of the Flies* tell about human nature and how societies are formed.

Sample 1 Score

I like survivor on tv and it reminds me of that book about the boys who were the lords of the flies. In the book, boys have to come together to live on an island which is like castaway. In survivor they are put on an iland to survive too. I think the show is cool and the boys in the book destroy everyone!

That is my essay on the survivor show and lord of the flies

383. Using a specific literary work, explain how a novel might influence change in society.

Sample 6 Score

Have you ever read a story that ultimately changed the way in which you thought about the world?

So often we form our opinions and lifestyles from our families and what we observe around us. Could it be possible that a novel might change the way in people's thinking? After reading Harper Lee's *To Kill A Mockingbird*, I realized for the first time how complex racism was, and the necessity for societal change.

I have always been aware of cultural and racial differences in others. I was raised to accept people for their differences and judge people solely on their character. However, I wasn't aware of the problems encountered by black people in the Deep South during the 1940s. In her novel, Lee makes it apparent that the color of skin was a determinant of social stature, no matter your character.

I felt that having a first person narrator, told from the perspective of a young girl in the South was a brilliant way to tell this story. Scout is at the age where she is only beginning to understand how society handles diversity and cultural differences. A black man, Tom Robinson, is accused of raping a white woman, even though none of the evidence points to him. For example, the narrator is a young girl named Scout. Her father, Atticus

Finch, is a well-respected, highly moral lawyer who is defending Tom. Even though Atticus finds evidence contrary to the accusations, he has no hope of winning this trial. Scout fights a boy in her class who tells her that her father is defending a "(racial slur)". Scout now begins to come to terms with her assumptions about people.

An interesting point is made in this novel. While the white people of this small town in Alabama discuss the horrors of Hitler persecuting Jewish people, Scout wonders how the same people could not understand that the white people of her town were doing the same to the blacks. This sends a powerful message to the reader through such a vivid analogy.

This novel elicits the reader to think about race relations and social bigotry. There are decent, moral black characters in this novel that are doomed because of their skin color. However, Lee portrays low class white families, such as Bob's, undeserving of respect, but able to live on a much higher social stature than the blacks. When Tom Robinson is killed escaping from prison, the town barely takes notice.

Through Lee's novel, society is faced with the vulgarities of race and social class, along with the racism of this Southern town. Her message that neither race nor class, but actions, define someone's character leave the reader with important social issues to be re-examined.

Sample 4 Score

In Harper Lee's novel *To Kill A Mockingbird*, many racial issues are brought into the story for the reader to think about. I think Lee does a nice job of bringing these issues to light.

Atticus Finch, a white lawyer, defending Tom Robinson, a black man accused of raping a white woman, sees that he has no chance of winning this case in this small Southern town, set in the 1940's. Finch's daughter, Scout, tells the story. I liked how Lee used Scout to tell the story, because it was from a child's point of view. Scout must face prejudiced people in the novel who make fun of her father for taking this case, even though her father is respected.

Many things in the novel make the reader feel horrible for the treatment of black people in this town. None of the evidence points to Tom, and even when he is shot at the end of the novel, no one seems to even care.

I really believe because of this book, that many people's ideas about race have been changed. I think that people should be treated with respect no matter the color of their skin.

Sample 1 Score

In this essay, I will write about how a book can change peeple's mind. If you ever read To Kill A Mockingbird, you would see why. A small girl tells this stiory and a black man is being in court because people think he rapped a wehite woman. The reader no's this isn't true, but the town in the south don't believe him. When I read this I was sad because of the way people get picked on. This is my essay on changing society. Thank you.

384. The theme of a literary piece is the central idea or message that it delivers. Cite a specific literary work and discuss the theme.

Sample 6 Score

Theme is the underlying message an author presents to his or her audience. Many times the theme of a work is apparent. Often we ask ourselves upon completing a novel, "What did that character learn at the end?" We base our judgment of characters on our cultural beliefs and emotions we experience in our lives. In Herman Hesse's *Siddartha*, the theme seems apparent—fulfillment in life through spiritual peace.

The main character, Siddartha, takes the reader on his life's journey to find truth and meaning in life. He decides to leave home with his childhood friend, Govinda. The setting of this story is India, with the social caste system as the motivation for his journey. Siddartha realizes that he yearns for more knowledge and understanding; far more that his father can provide him with. He seeks spiritual fulfillment and wisdom. Even though this story is set in India, the theme is universal. Just as many of us decide to go on to college to learn more about the world, and ourselves; Siddartha does the same.

At different stages of his journey he acquires wisdom, learns as much as he can, and forges on to new experiences. Siddartha is not unlike a person today in our culture. Many of us challenge ourselves with new ideas and experiences. Sometimes we fail, other times we succeed. However, what unifies us is the desire to explore the unknown. The trade-off is we may discover we are much happier after taking those risks, than if we never ventured out. This is the theme in *Siddartha*. It is the message that is universal. In fact, there is a very popular book out now about moving cheese. It is a metaphor for the same theme as in *Siddartha*. Moving out of our comfort zones into a new, unfamiliar arena, hoping to find what it is we are looking for.

Siddartha goes through both pleasant and unpleasant experiences in this novel. At one point, he acquires incredible wealth and has every material possession he could ever dream of. However, at this point in his life, he contemplates suicide! He has become so gluttonous that he sickens himself. He realizes material possessions cannot bring him peace. From this scene, the theme of attaining spiritual peace is strengthened. How many times have we come across people with enormous wealth, but little peace and fulfillment in their lives?

Siddartha is a great novel and its theme is apparent. The quest for spiritual peace, wisdom, and self-understanding is unpredictable, but attainable through the trials of life and what it has to offer.

Sample 4 Score

The theme of a literary work is the main idea, or message that we understand. Many times the theme is not stated directly, but the reader can usually figure it out. One particular novel I enjoyed reading was Siddartha by Herman Hesse. In this novel, a young man begins his life's journey towards spirituality and understanding. This is a common theme in literature.

While Siddartha is still a young man, he asks his father to explain certain things to him about life and religion. His father doesn't have all the answers for him, so Siddartha decides to leave home and try to find the answers for himself. He brings along his friend Govinda. This book takes place in India; that is the reason for the unfamiliar names. Siddartha and his friend encounter many new people and experiences.

Towards the end of his journey, Siddartha has discovered many things about himself. He realizes that possessions cannot make him happy. He becomes aware that true happiness and peace are found inside.

This theme is very common in literature. I think this is true because people everywhere go through what Siddartha did sometime in their life.

Sample 1 Score

Theme is where you can tell what a writer is thinking about. I think that sometimes writers like to fool with people and guess real hard to see if they can understand.

In Siddartha, a book about a boy who tries to see about life, I think the theme is about a boy in India who likes to go on trips and helps people.

That is my essay about theme. I hope you liked this essay.

387. Compare/contrast the fear of terrorism and the concern with safety issues in present day society with George Orwell's novel, *1984.*

Sample 6 Score

The events of September 11th shattered our belief that we as Americans are immune to terrorism and its proponents. Our society has taken for granted security and free will. However, heightened measures have been taken in public arenas to bolster our safety. With this heightened security comes the forfeiture of some civil liberties that George Orwell wrote about in his novel *1984*.

In his novel, Orwell was writing from the perspective of nation that recently endured a world war. Orwell wrote his novel in 1948, and simply rotated the last two digits in the year to explore what the world might be like in the future. In this world that Orwell writes about, the government has surveillance in every imaginable public space. There is also a law enforcement collaborative called the "thought police." In this society, no one could have anti-governmental sentiment whether vocalized or internalized. If you violated this law, "Big Brother" took you away. This government, (Big Brother), supposedly gave the citizens what they needed in order to survive. In this cold, mundane society, there was always a camera somewhere watching you. I think it is appropriate to assume that this society was under Communist rule, and Orwell was indeed frightening his readers to the thought of such a threat. This threat was very significant in the times this novel was written. Orwell was conveying the themes of manipulation of the truth and loss of identity. In our present day society, there are many parallels to Orwell's novel.

Since September 11th, our government has taken steps in order to tighten security and minimize terrorist attacks. By the same token, members of our society must forfeit certain civil liberties. For example, if you travel by air now, you must arrive extremely early before departure, your belongings are scrutinized more closely, and you may have to be patted down or asked to remove your shoes. These actions seem to be intrusive, but most people will accept them to ensure safety.

Furthermore, it is becoming commonplace to find video cameras in many public arenas. Many airports, stores, and offices install cameras for surveillance. Technology has produced cameras that are so small, they can be installed in a shirt or jacket button. Many parents install cameras in their homes to monitor activity if they must leave and hire a sitter. Many police vehicles are equipped with video recorders so that the tape might yield evidence in court. There are even popular television shows that air actual surveillance tapes. This is eerily reminiscent of what occurs in Orwell's *1984*.

Although we have no thought police, nor do we live under totalitarian rule, our society has definitely surrendered its privacy in order to protect its freedom. Orwell seemed to understand how technology can influence society and its freedoms.

Sample 4 Score

George Orwell seems to understand how our society can become disconnected from one another.

I believe since the terrorist attacks, that our sense of security has been compromised. We now have surveillance in almost every aspect of life.

In Orwell's *1984*, the society he writes about is very similar to what I have learned about Communism. In this society, there is a dictator and his officials. No one in this society can think for themselves or think anything anti-government. If you do, then the "thought police" will come and get you. Also, there are cameras everywhere in the city. This is similar to what our society is going through now.

Since the terror attacks, our government leaders have asked us to be on alert and to endure tighter restrictions while in public places. For example, you may have to take off your shoes in the airport now, since a terrorist was caught on a plane trying to light a fuse in his sneaker that contained explosives.

Also, if you go to a store like 7-11 or Macy's, you can always find a camera looking at you. I personally feel frightened when I see a camera everywhere, but it just might be helpful to catch people who break the law.

I don't believe that our society will become like Orwell's society in 1984, but I do feel that camera surveillance and checkpoints are very similar to the plot in his novel.

Sample 1 Score

In 1984, people have no privacy because the powers to be want to know what they think and how they act. This reminds me of what happens today. I went in to a store and tried to buy some snacks. A man behind the counter started to scream at me because he thought he saw me stealing something.

Also, my dad flies, and he says that is hard now because all the people check everything you have and they pat you down like in the movies. I don't think this is fair and it reminds me of Orwells story.

390. Personification is the technique wherein a non-human character is given human thoughts, feelings, and dialogue. Illustrate how this technique is used in your favorite novel or short story.

Sample 6 Score

Personification is a clever technique wherein non-human characters are given human characteristics. Using this technique, the reader is able to understand how an animal feels, or what a tree is thinking, or even the most intimate thoughts of an old pair of sneakers! Rudyard Kipling's "Rikki-Tikki-Tavi" is one of my favorite short stories. In it, all of the animals are personified, which is crucial because the protagonist is a mongoose.

Rikki-Tikki-Tavi is a small mongoose who nearly drowns after a flood sweeps him away from his home. A boy named Teddy finds the mongoose, and he and his mother nurse the animal back to health. Rikki never converses in English with his human family, however he does interact with the other animals in the garden, speaking in English. I find this technique to be helpful in formulating the plot. For example, a mongoose's natural enemy is the cobra. Kipling uses these two enemies in the wild and makes them the protagonist and antagonist of the short story. Throughout the story, Rikki-Tikki finds himself battling adversaries in the garden in an effort to save Teddy's family.

This story follows the archetype of the battle between good and evil. If we look closely at the plot, biblical themes are apparent. Snakes in the garden may remind some of the biblical story of Adam and Eve. Without personification in this biblical story, Eve might not have been tempted if the serpent didn't have the ability to speak. Although Rikki-Tikki cannot converse with the humans in the story, the reader is able to understand his character and his thoughts. For example, before he battles Nag, the male antagonist serpent, he is cautious and a bit nervous. However, he won't show his fear to his enemy. Only the reader understands Rikki's character from this point of view.

Rudyard Kipling was clever enough to observe what occurs in nature, blending it with personification, and creating a timeless story of good versus evil.

Sample 4 Score

Personification is the technique where the author gives non-human characters human thoughts, speech, and feelings. I like how this is used in Rudyard Kipling's Rikki-Tikki-Tavi.

Without personification, the main character, who is a mongoose, would not be able to express his feelings. The story would need a narrator, like the kind you see on television's Wild Discovery. Some of those documentaries show animals in the wild, while a narrator tells the audience why the animals behave certain ways. With personification, a non-fictional event can be fictionalized.

For example, a mongoose's natural enemy in the wild is the cobra. In Rikki-Tikki-Tavi, the mongoose is the hero, while the cobra is the villain. Both animals have conversations with other animals and the reader can see what they are thinking about. Rikki-Tikki is nervous to fight the cobras, but doesn't show it when he starts to battle. I like how the author lets the story unfold through personification.

Although Rikki can't talk with his human family, he behaves like a family pet. When the cobras plot to kill the family, Rikki defends them by killing the snakes. This story follows the common theme of good versus evil. Without personification, the story would not be so enjoyable.

Sample 1 Score

Personification sounds like person, and that is what it means. When a writer gives something words and feelings, it is called personification. In this essay, I will tell you about personification.

Rikki-Tikki is a animul who can talk and have conersashuns with other animuls. He fights snakes and wins! When I read this story I like how animus can talk because then I can see how they feel and stuff.

This is my essay on animuls and talking.

395. Many times in Shakespeare's plays, the setting changes from rural or pastoral to urban. Compare and contrast these settings. Explain the reason for the shift of scenery, using support from specific plays.

Sample 6 Score

Many times in Shakespeare's works, the setting changes from a city to a pastoral venue. Although change in setting is expected, there is an underlying reason why he chooses these specific areas. In his play *A Midsummer Night's Dream*, the setting changes from the city of Athens to a forest near the city. The characters behave very differently in each setting.

The play deals with marriages, love, family, and non-conformity. The Duke of Athens is about to be married to a woman who he recently defeated in war. Another element of the plot deals with a young woman whose father is demanding she marry a man she is not in love with. The woman decides to run away to the forest with the man she does love. There are two distinct settings here and I believe Shakespeare was mirroring human nature in the change of scenery. Often when someone is faced with a pressing problem or decision, they will retreat either physically to a quiet place to meditate, or they might go out with friends in order to take release from the issue or problem. Similarly in this play, the forest is viewed as a place of "non-reality," or a dream world. Fairies and supernatural beings inhabit the forest. This is a place of refuge that contrasts the conformity of the city. There are, however, similarities in both settings.

Just as the Duke of Athens is marrying Hippolyta, there is King Oberon and his queen in the forest. Both couples are learning about the trials of love. There are colorful characters in both venues that keep the audience entertained also. One such character who lives in the forest is Puck. Puck is a fairy-type character who plays tricks on the characters and ultimately tries to teach them lessons throughout the play. One of the more famous lines from Shakespeare is found in this work when Puck states, "Oh what fools these mortals be." There are lessons to be learned in both the city and the forest, but the forest is more of a dream world or an escape from reality.

Shakespeare cleverly changes the setting in this play to expose human folly and lends keen insight into human nature.

Sample 4 Score

The change in setting in Shakespeare's *A Midsummer Night's Dream* is used to show contrast between a world of conformity and court life with a dream type world. Shakespeare does this to highlight human nature.

In this play, there are two different worlds. One is the city of Athens where the Duke is about to be married. The city has its strict rules and conformity. One part of the plot deals with a woman who doesn't want to marry the man her father wants her to. She decides to run away to the forest with the man she loves. The forest is now seen as an escape from reality. In the forest, there are fairies and other supernatural beings. People also do this in real life. If someone is sad, they may go down to the beach to think or just to be alone.

There is a similarity in both worlds though. There is the Duke of Athens in the city, and there is King Oberon in the forest. They both are involved with their marriages and try to help others with their problems.

I think Shakespeare does a great job using the city and the forest in this play to show two sides of human nature.

Sample 1 Score

In this essay I will talk about shakespeare's play a midsummer night's dream and how this play uses the setting. The setting is the place where things happened. I think the woods and the city are good places for this play. One place is nice, but full of fairies and weird stuff. The city is more like real life and has real people. this is the difference of the setting in the play.

412. A third type of conflict is called character vs. him/herself. This is also referred to as internal conflict, because the character must face self-inflicted fears and problems. Write about this type of conflict, using a piece of literature that you have read.

Sample 6 Score

In many literary works there is a central conflict. Conflict can occur in many ways. There is character versus another character, character versus an outside force like nature, and internal conflict, where a character must battle themselves mentally and emotionally. Often these types of conflicts can occur simultaneously in a literary work. I have chosen to discuss my favorite type of conflict in one of my favorite plays by Shakespeare; *Hamlet*.

Internal conflict is the most intricate of all the types of conflict. We may read about a character that must physically defend themselves against another character. Also, there are many characters that have to brave the elements and survive in life-threatening situations. For example, Ishmael, the narrator and sole survivor in Herman Melville's *Moby Dick* tells the story of the giant white whale. But the most intense is internal conflict. In Shakespeare's *Hamlet*, a young prince must battle his conscience.

Hamlet, the main character, has recently lost his father. While he is still mourning, his mother marries his father's brother, Claudius. However, Hamlet's father's ghost appears to him and shows him the foul play that surrounded his death. Hamlet learns that his uncle actually murdered his father! This is where internal conflict is most present. In one of the most famous Shakespearian lines, Hamlet ponders, "To be, or not to be . . . ". Hamlet must now decide whether to take action and avenge his father's death, or to remain passive. This decision weighs so heavily on his conscience, that others notice a drastic change in his behavior. Hamlet must decide if being passive is the equivalent of being a coward. Eventually, this play comes to a tragic end, and Hamlet decides to avenge his father's murder.

I believe that internal conflict works ideally in literature. Of course, Shakespeare presents Hamlet's internal conflict through soliloquy, and this was performed on stage, but when you are able to read what a person is struggling through, you can more closely relate to the character. Internal conflict conjures up the fears that many of us have in everyday life. Hopefully ours are not as tragic as Hamlets were!

Sample 4 Score

Conflict is what makes literature interesting to read. If there were no problems, then the reader might become bored. One type of conflict is called internal conflict. This type occurs when a character is battling their conscience. One such character that experiences this is Hamlet from one of Shakespeare's most famous plays.

In *Hamlet*, the main character (by the same name), has just lost his father in a war. His father was the king of Denmark, and Hamlet is prince. Hamlet is visited by his father's ghost and shown that his death was murder by Hamlet's own uncle! This puts Hamlet in a really bad spot. Now he must decide whether to seek revenge for his father's death or do nothing. Why would he do nothing? Well, his uncle is marrying his mother now. Hamlet has the toughest time trying to decide whether seek revenge. The famous quote "To be or not to be . . ." shows his internal conflict.

Hamlet does seek revenge, but I like how Shakespeare shows what a character is thinking and what goes on in their minds. Internal conflict adds interest for audiences.

Sample 1 Score

In this essay I will talk about what is internal conflict. In many works of writers, a person has thoughts that lead them to make choices. You can tell what that person is thinking by reading. Hamlet had one where he did not like his uncle and his dad was ded. Hamlet had to get even with his dads killers or do nothing. So Hamlet had a hard time trying to make up his mind.

I think that internal conflict is when you have a problem that needs to have solved.

416. Discuss a piece of literature in which the author is also the narrator. Describe the way he or she uses actual events from his or her life in his or her writing.

Sample 6 Score

In literature, there are varying points of view in relaying the events. If the narrator was actually part of the events, this is called first-person narration. When the narrator is merely telling a story, but was not part of the events, this is third-person narration. At times, a reader might be thankful that the narrator is only telling a story as the events unfold, especially if the main characters are in some sort of danger. I personally enjoy first-person narration because you are allowed into the mind of the main character. This was especially enjoyable while reading J.D. Salinger's *Catcher in the Rye*.

The main character, Holden Caufield, is the narrator as well. He is a very complex character who doesn't seem to fit in socially. Salinger creates the world from Holden's point of view. Although Holden seems apathetic towards many things in his life such as his schoolwork and friends, he is a deeply sensitive character marred by his view of the world. For example, in the beginning of the novel, Holden questions why his roommates are so popular and can converse so well, especially with members of the opposite sex. His insecurities are revealed so that the reader can explore his character and perhaps identify with him. If Salinger had written this as a third-person narration, the reader might not understand Holden's character as well.

Even though Holden Caufield is a tragic character, and many of his actions are not the most beneficial, Salinger allows us to identify with Holden's insecurities and private dealings, many of which the reader might identify with.

Sample 4 Score

When the author is involved in the action in a book, it is called first person narration. This is my favorite type of narration because you can understand what goes on in a character's mind. A good example is J.D. Salinger's *Catcher in the Rye*.

The story is told from the viewpoint of the main character, Holden Caufield. He is a very shy, withdrawn young man who is also sensitive. He sometimes wonders if he is like other people, and he is trying to find himself. I think many readers can identify with Holden from time to time. I think everyone feels insecure at one time or another.

I think that Salinger chooses the narrator for this novel well. If this was written any other way, we might not sympathize with the main character as much.

Sample 1 Score

I think 1st person narrator is a nice way to tell a story. In this essay you will hear about this narrator.

In cather in the Rye, I forget the author, the story is told by the main character, Hulden. His is a boy who is afraid of everything! I can feel the way he did sometimes.

This is why I like the narrator person one.

431. The *coming of age* theme is very popular in literature. This term refers to a pre-adolescent boy or girl going through many difficult, life altering experiences in order to reach young adulthood. Using a novel you are familiar with, discuss this theme. Be sure to use supporting details and evidence in your essay.

Sample 6 Score

The theme "coming of age" is a common one, where an adolescent boy or girl is faced with decisions that ultimately lead them into adulthood. *Barn Burning*, by William Faulkner, embodies this theme with messages of family loyalty and morality.

The story is set in the South, roughly thirty years after the Civil War. The main character who comes of age is Sarty Snopes, an adolescent whose father, Ab Snopes is a poor sharecropper frustrated by the post-Civil War Aristocracy. Sarty's father is a very destructive, immoral character. In the South at this time, if a person wanted to deliver the most potent form of revenge against their neighbor, they would have someone burn their barn down. This crude assault makes perfect sense considering the main income providing lot was agriculture and livestock. If a person lost their barn where these things were stored, their lives would ultimately be ruined. Ab and his son drift from place to place, and Ab makes money as a hired "hit" for barns. His son is deeply troubled by his father's destructiveness, but follows along out of "blood," or the loyalty of family regardless of the activities.

Throughout the novel, Sarty is faced with internal conflict. He knows that his father is doing something highly illegal and immoral; however, he wishes to remain loyal to family. Faulkner explores this coming of age theme with real depth and conviction, as the boy struggles with his conscience.

The climax of this novel comes when the boy and his father are taken in by a warm, friendly man who provides the two with meals, lodging, and conversation. Sarty takes a genuine liking to the man; however, he knows that his father plans to burn the man's barn down. Although he tries to convince his father not to commit this heinous act, Ab takes the boy in the middle of the night towards the barn. Sarty makes the hardest decision of his life and warns the man. In the closing scene, a gunshot is heard and the reader can assume that the father has been caught and killed. Sarty has crossed the threshold of pre-adolescence and has deceived "blood" in order to preserve his morality.

William Faulkner's *Barn Burning* is a remarkable story of coming of age, where a boy must make the ultimate decision and thus becomes a man.

Sample 4 Score

Barn Burning, by William Faulkner, is a great story that has the theme coming of age. In this story, a young boy must decide whether to follow his father in committing unlawful acts, or listen to his own conscience.

Barn Burning takes place in the South, after the Civil War. The boy, Sarty Snopes, and his father, Ab, travel from place to place, hired to burn down barns. Ab is a sharecropper who is angry at the society of the South. During this time, it was the worst thing you could do to someone, burning down their barn. This is where a person would make all of their money, so it was the ultimate slap in the face if you wanted revenge on someone. Sarty doesn't like what his dad does, but stays with him because it's his family duty. He is conflicted on whether to follow hi father or do what he knows is right.

Sarty and his dad are taken in by a man on a plantation and treated very nicely. Sarty begins to really like this man, however he knows that his father is planning to burn down his barn. Sarty is faced with turning in his father or being loyal. In the end, he turns his dad in and this is where he finally comes of age. I think this was a very powerful story.

Sample 1 Score

In this essay, I will tell you about to come to age in Barn Burning. This story was wen a man and his son burn barns, but the boy does not want to do it. He tries to think about what is right, but he wants to stick with blood. His family should not snitch. Barn burning was very bad in this time near the civil war, so The boy at the end turns in his father and becomes a man. That is my essay on barn Burning.

447. Discuss how the reader might sympathize with the main character in Christopher Marlowe's *Dr. Faustus*, even though he sells his soul to the Devil.

Sample 6 Score

The familiar adage about selling one's soul to the devil conjures up two distinct images—dabbling with the occult and being granted magical gifts.

Although most people would not want to or would not dare to cross into such dangerous territory, Dr. John Faustus, the renowned scholar in this Elizabethan tragedy, could not resist.

Christopher Marlowe, author of *Dr. Faustus*, created a complex character in the play of the same name. This character is tragic, foolish, ambitious, intelligent, and pitied. For all the good and bad traits he has, the audience cannot help but share in Faustus' regret at the end of the play.

Faustus has mastered many disciplines and is a well-known scholar. However, he yearns for more knowledge beyond the realm of what is offered. Faustus summons the occult and encounters a demon named Mephistopheles, a servant to Lucifer. Faustus makes an offer to give his soul to the devil in exchange for twenty-four years of magic. Mephistopheles tries to dissuade Faustus from such a fate, but Faustus persists until the deal has been made. Once this occurs, Faustus is ready to satisfy his ambitions.

At this point in the play, the audience—although apprehensive about Faustus' choice—is just as curious as he was about magic and infinite knowledge. Faustus wants to learn the secrets of the universe. He also wants a wife. Basically, he desires the things that most humans desire, and this is where Marlowe captures the audience's empathy. We know that what Faustus has done is immoral and tragic, but we want to share in this display of power as he entertains courts by summoning historical spirits. The audience has pity for Faustus when he has bouts with his conscience. For example, at one point he prays desperately to God for forgiveness, but the audience realizes that no matter how desperate or how much he pleads, the devil will make sure the contract is honored. What is particularly powerful at the end of the play is the torment and desperation Faustus experiences as he fights the clock and tries to hold back time. But, the hours and minutes close in on his fate. Colleagues find his body the next day, and the audience realizes that he has been dragged down to hell.

Although the audience can blame Faustus for summoning the occult and bringing this tragedy on himself, Marlowe creates such a complex character that he is to be pitied for his choices.

Sample 4 Score

Christopher Marlowe creates a character that can be both loathed for his attitude, but also pitied for his choices in *Dr. Faustus*.

In this play, a young doctor with a lot of knowledge desires more from his studies. He realizes he can't get this knowledge from earth, so he summons the help of the devil. The devil's servant, Mephistopheles, tries to convince Faustus that this is something he should not play around with. Faustus is persistent, so the deal with the devil is finally sealed in blood.

Faustus enjoys his newly found powers, such as bringing up spirits. He does however have bouts with his conscience about his choices. The audience feels pity for him because we would want his power, but we definitely don't want his fate. He tries to bargain and pray, but it is no use. The devil finally wins at the end, and we feel sorrowful for Faustus.

In conclusion, even though Faustus does something that he knows he shouldn't have, the audience still feels pity for him when he has to trade in his soul.

Sample 1 Score

The devil in the play Docter Faust plays a trick on him because he wants to be smarter. I think that Faust is a good man that does wrong.

In the play he has magic but this does not help the devil or make Faust a smart man. He must go to hell when this is done, so he feels sorry for hisself. The people who watch the play fell bad for him to. Oh, well, he made his choice in life and now he is doomd.

453. Discuss a hero in a literary piece that you have read.

Sample 6 Score

In her autobiographical novel, *I Know Why The Caged Bird Sings*, Maya Angelou relates her story as a poor black girl living in racially segregated Stamps, Arkansas. As the story unfolds, she describes relationships with her family and members of the community, her love of reading, her feeling of inequality, the racial prejudice she suffers, and her experiences as a single mother. What makes Angelou heroic, I think, is her perseverance over a multitude of odds.

In the beginning of the novel, the reader learns that Angelou is living with her grandmother because her birth mother abandoned her. With no direction or positive influence in her life, a white woman introduced her to "her first white love" – William Shakespeare –who befriended Angelou. Reading became an escape from her reality. In real life, she weathered many hardships on her path to adulthood. What then makes Angelou a hero?

The archetype of a hero usually involves hardship, struggle, and an arduous journey. When this hero reaches a certain breaking point or climactic scene, a turn of events usually brings about resolution, self-awareness, and peace. This is true in Angelou's autobiography.

Throughout the novel, racial prejudice is an overriding factor in her life. Even though Angelou documents her struggles against prejudice, lack of a formal education, and personal failure, she comes full circle when her son is born. She embarks on a new self-awareness and peace. There is a heroic quality about a woman who has overcome so many odds.

Although Angelou is both author and subject, she embodies the spirit of a heroic character who ultimately prevailed against the odds.

Sample 4 Score

An hero in my opinion is the author Maya Angelou. Often people think of heroes as sports stars or world leaders, but Maya Angelou is a hero.

In Maya's book, *I know why the caged bird Sings*, Maya is really the main character. In fact, this is an autobiography of her life. In the book she goes through many hard times and has tough choices to make. The town she is from is in Arkansas, and it is a very racially divided town. Her grandmother is also raising her. One thing that Angelou loves to do is read. She meets a woman who shows her how to read, and well!

I think she is a hero because she survived being a victim. Angelou was treated poorly because of her race, she was raped by a relative, abandoned by her mother, and becomes a mother herself. Similar to a hero, she has to be brave and strong-willed.

I think Maya Angelou is a great person and a true hero.

Sample 1 Score

A hero is a person who is in comic books and things, but did you know something about Miya Angeloo?

She is a writer and she came from being very poor to becoming a success. In this essay I will talk abot angeloo.

Well, maya had problems because some poeple are rasist, but she made her problems beter and even rote about them. And I think she is very nice and brave i hope everyone reads about this strong hero.

465. Write a literary analysis of a Robert Frost poem. Include theme and symbolism in your discussion.

Sample 6 Score

Robert Frost's comforting, sad, and often poignant poetry is usually filled with metaphors and vivid imagery. Perhaps my favorite Frost poem is "Stopping by Woods on a Snowy Evening." The imagery creates a memorable portrait of the beauty and power of nature.

Near the beginning, the narrator is introduced as a working man, who has stopped to rest: "My little horse must think it queer / To stop without a farmhouse near." The narrator suggests that his days are mostly spent in labor, moving from place to place. On a whim, he stops riding to watch the "woods fill up with snow." During this brief moment, the narrator achieves spiritual transcendence and peace as he connects with nature.

Throughout the poem, the narrator's horse is a symbol of daily labor and the constant struggle of civilization. Taken from the wilds of nature, domesticated, and trained to obey orders, the horse no longer has any appreciation of nature. While the narrator relaxes in the woods, his horse "gives his harness bells a shake / To ask if there is some mistake." The irony here is that the man becomes even more connected to nature than the once-wild beast he rides.

It's important that this event takes place during "The darkest evening of the year" because the darkness allows the narrator to be hidden from the civilized and unnatural world he lives in every day. At the same time, the darkness of the evening is ironic because the narrator can't really see the beauty of the woods very clearly. In this way, Frost suggests that nature's beauty is more than just visual. It's spiritual too. In the "lovely, dark and deep" woods, the narrator is able to fully appreciate the beauty of nature without seeing it.

After his brief moment of peace, the narrator must return to the working world. The line, "And miles to go before I sleep" is repeated at the end to show how weary and tired the narrator has become. Here, the "miles" represent long spans of time. He has a long time to wait before he gets home that night, and he also has a long time to wait before he reaches the ultimate sleep of death. But in this poem, the idea of death isn't negative because when the narrator dies, he will finally be permanently reunited with the beauty of nature.

Sample 4 Score

Robert Frost's poem "Stopping By Woods On A Snowy Evening" can be interpreted as a man learning to appreciate nature.

The poem starts out as a man in a horse-drawn carriage stops to appreciate the serenity of a dark, snowy evening. Although this might seem to be a simple poem using imagery, Frost sends a message about the power of nature. The man seems to enjoy the woods even more than his horse, who was probably born in the woods. It's a dark evening but somehow the man can still appreciate the lovely forest.

At the end of the poem, Frost says that he can't stop to rest anymore because he has things to do. I thought this part was really sad because the man seemed so tired and didn't want to leave.

This poem has many symbolic elements in it and I enjoyed this very much.

Sample 1 Score

Roburt frost has made a poem about a snowy evening. In this essay I will explain about the message in the poem I have read.

The poem is about a man who goes into a cold forest and stops to watch snow. I like to snowboard in the winter, so I know what he is felling. Afterwards, frost says he cannot stop anymore because he has to go into town and help people. This is my intreputashun of his poem.

483. Compare the society of *The Scarlet Letter* to our society today. Compare and contrast how Hester Prynne would have been treated today with how she was treated in the novel.

Sample 6 Score

Hester Prynne, from Nathaniel Hawthorne's *The Scarlet Letter,* would not necessarily have fared much better today than in her own time. Some of the Puritanical influences in Salem, Massachusetts at that time still exist in modern society. Public ridicule remains an integral part of our culture, infidelity is still deplored, and unfortunately, women are still often seen as the more guilty party of any extramarital affair.

In *The Scarlet Letter,* Reverend Dimmsdale is a spiritual leader of the community. However, he impregnates a young woman named Hester Prynne, who believes her husband has died at sea. As a result of their affair, Hester is forced to wear a scarlet "A" on her chest and stand in the midst of the town on a scaffold. Meanwhile, Dimmsdale keeps his distance and remains silent out of fear. In modern times, it would be hard to imagine anyone who has had an affair being forced to wear a red letter on his or her clothes for all to see, but, at the same time, public ridicule has become a part of modern culture as well. Celebrities are publically ridiculed on the covers of tabloid magazines every day, and the details of their private lives are frequently broadcast on shows like *Access Hollywood.* In our society, extramarital affairs have become public knowledge. From celebrities to politicians, one way or another, affairs make news and sell papers.

Also, in the book, Hester Prynne is unfairly singled out as the guilty one as a result of Dimmesdale's silence. Even now, it is often the woman who is viewed as the immoral one with poor judgment. Although Dimmesdale finally delivers a powerful sermon toward the end of the novel, confessing to the affair before his congregation, he dies—rather conveniently—shortly after, thereby escaping any punishment or public ridicule. So, in the end, Hester Prynne may not have been treated much better in our times. For its portrayal of this timeless situation, *The Scarlet Letter* remains a viable novel.

Sample 4 Score

Our society views women the same as in Nathaniel Hawthorne's Scarlet Letter. It's very interesting how things change very little in such a wide span of time. Hester Prynne is brought in front of the town on a scaffold for having an affair and becoming pregnant. Her husband is assumed lost at sea, however the townspeople scorn her and exclude her from society. She is made to wear a letter A on her clothes for embarrassment. Although sometimes women who have affairs are treated badly, they don't ever have to wear scarlet letters anymore.

Reverend Dimmsdale is never really looked at badly, even though at the end he confesses. It's the same today. Usually, there is one person who is viewed as the bad guy, and one person who is innocent, even though both people are having the affair. It's the same sort of thing you read in the newspapers with celebrities and politicians, it seems someone is always having an affair. For all these reasons, I think that what happens in the book is mostly the same as what would happen in modern times.

Sample 1 Score

Hester in the scarlet letter was a women who had had an afair with an importent man and she was made fun because of it. She had to where an A letter to show she was sorry. Everyne in the town didnt like her becase they think she did something very bad and they also were not mean to the man. I wouldnt treet poeple like that along time ago today or in the futur either.

ALSO IN THE
SKILL BUILDER IN FOCUS
SERIES

501 Quantitative Comparison Questions
ISBN: 1-57685-434-5 ■ 224 pages ■ 7 x 10

501 Math Word Problems
ISBN: 1-57685-439-6 ■ 224 pages ■ 7 x 10

501 Vocabulary
ISBN: 1-57685-465-5 ■ 224 pages ■ 7 x 10

501 Sentence Completion Questions
ISBN: 1-57685-511-2 ■ 192 pages ■ 7 x 10

501 Critical Reading Questions
ISBN: 1-57685-510-4 ■ 256 pages ■ 7 x 10

Master these skills and score higher!

Achieve maximum results with proven practice

Build test-taking confidence—fast

**Great for the SAT, GRE, GMAT—
and other standardized tests**

Focus *FAST* on the Skills You Need
to Pass the Test

SKILL BUILDER IN FOCUS

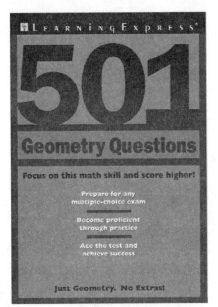

LEARNINGEXPRESS

501

Geometry Questions

Focus on this math skill and score higher!

Prepare for any
multiple-choice exam

Become proficient
through practice

Ace the test and
achieve success

Just Geometry. No Extras!

ISBN: 1-57685-425-6
288 pages
7 x 10

---

501 Geometry Questions

Master this math skill and score higher!

Achieve maximum results with proven practice

Build test-taking confidence—fast

**Great for the SAT, GRE, GMAT—
and other standardized tests**

**Learn math concepts and properties,
including trigonometry basics**

**Work with angles and lines, identify shapes,
determine ratios, proportion, perimeter,
and surface measures**

**Assess your true geometry competency level
and put yourself on the path to improvement**

Focus *FAST* on Geometry

LearningExpress

SKILL BUILDER IN FOCUS

LearningExpress®

501

Algebra Questions

Focus on this math skill and score higher!

Prepare for any
multiple-choice exam

Become proficient
through practice

Ace the test and
achieve success

Just Algebra. No Extras!

ISBN: 1-57685-424-8
288 pages
7 x 10

501 Algebra Questions

Master this math skill and score higher!

Achieve maximum results with proven practice

Build test-taking confidence—fast

**Great practice for the SAT, GRE, GMAT—
and other standardized tests**

Learn math concepts and properties

Work with algebraic expressions and integers

**Multiply and factor polynomials, use quadratic
formulas, and avoid careless mistakes**

**Assess your true algebra competency level
and put yourself on the path to improvement**

Focus *FAST* on Algebra

SKILL BUILDER IN FOCUS

LearningExpress

501

Synonym & Antonym Questions

Focus on this vocabulary skill and score higher!

Prepare for any
multiple-choice exam

Become proficient
through practice

Ace the test and
achieve success

Just Synonyms and Antonyms. No Extras!

ISBN: 1-57685-4423-X
128 pages
7 x 10

501 Synonym & Antonym Questions

Master this vocabulary skill and score higher!

Achieve maximum results with proven practice

Build test-taking confidence—fast

**Great for the SAT, GRE, GMAT—
and other standardized tests**

**Start thinking of words in terms of other words
with similar or opposite meanings**

**Pinpoint exact word definitions and
become aware of secondary word meanings**

**Learn to switch gears from synonym questions to
antonym questions, avoiding careless mistakes**

**Assess your true vocabulary level and
put yourself on the path to improvement**

Focus *FAST* on Synonyms and Antonyms

SKILL BUILDER IN FOCUS

LearningExpress

501

Word Analogy Questions

Focus on this vocabulary skill and score higher!

Prepare for any
multiple-choice exam

Become proficient
through practice

Ace the test and
achieve success

Just Word Analogies! No Extras!

ISBN: 1-57685-422-1
128 pages
7 x 10

501 Word Analogy Questions

Master this logic and reasoning skill and score higher!

Achieve maximum results with proven practice

Build test-taking confidence—fast

Great for the SAT, GRE, GMAT—and other standardized tests

**Pinpoint exact word definitions and
become aware of secondary word meanings**

**Deduce the correct relationship between words and draw
logical conclusions about possible answer choices**

**Learn to identify types of analogies—cause/effect, part/whole,
type/category, synonym, antonym, word knowledge,
and more—to avoid careless mistakes**

**Assess your true ability to apply logic and reasoning skills to
word knowledge and put yourself on the path to improvement**

Focus *FAST* on Word Analogies